RECLAIM YOUR *life*

Dear Reader—

If this book happens to land in your hands, I pray it allows you to achieve everything you have ever desired in life — health, and all wealth, happiness, fulfillment, and all things you can ever imagine. God this on you in Jesus' name. I pray you and thank you for allowing me to go on this journey with you!

Your friend,
[signature]

RECLAIM YOUR *life*

JODI WATKINS

Copyright © 2020 by Jodi Watkins.

Library of Congress Control Number: 2020904863
ISBN: Hardcover 978-1-7960-9379-7
Softcover 978-1-7960-9378-0
eBook 978-1-7960-9377-3

All rights reserved. No part of this book may be reproduced or transmitted in any form or by any means, electronic or mechanical, including photocopying, recording, or by any information storage and retrieval system, without permission in writing from the copyright owner.

Unless otherwise noted, all Bible verses used in this book were taken from THE HOLY BIBLE, NEW INTERNATIONAL VERSION®, NIV® Copyright © 1973, 1978, 1984, 2011 by Biblica, Inc.™ Used by permission. All rights reserved worldwide.

Any people depicted in stock imagery provided by Getty Images are models, and such images are being used for illustrative purposes only.
Certain stock imagery © Getty Images.

Print information available on the last page.

Rev. date: 03/11/2020

To order additional copies of this book, contact:
Xlibris
1-888-795-4274
www.Xlibris.com
Orders@Xlibris.com
809462

CONTENTS

Acknowledgements ix
Preface xv
Introduction xix

Chapter 1: Mindset Development 1
   1.1 Stop Blaming Others 1
   1.2 Don't Dwell on the Past 4
   1.3 Take Ownership 6
   1.4 Believe in Yourself … You CAN DO THIS! 12

Chapter 2: Time Management 23
   2.1 Wake Up Earlier 23

Chapter 3: Self-Care and Positivity 37
   3.1 Stop Worrying About the Day as Soon as You Wake Up ... 37
   3.2 Say "Thank You" for Everything You Have 46

Chapter 4: Basic Nutrition 53
   4.1 Food Intake 53
   4.2 How to Eat 60
   4.3 Diary Tracking 61
   4.4 Intermittent Fasting 68
   4.5 Science Over Fads 73
   4.6 The Science and Why It Works 78

Chapter 5: Exercise 81
   5.1 Love the Feeling of Becoming Energized 81
   5.2 Have Balance Without Becoming Overwhelmed 83
   5.3 Being Wiser 84
   5.4 Why Strength Training is Important/Dispelling the Myths ... 86
   5.5. Creating an Action Plan 87

Chapter 6: Forming Habits Through Consistency 95
    6.1 Repeat and Practice 95
    6.2 Tell Your Story 97

Conclusion 103
Resources 105
Appendix – Worksheets for Continuation 107
    1.1 Worksheet 1 – Mindset/Feelings/Stress Management
        Worksheet 107
    1.2 Worksheet 2 – Time Management 113
    1.3 Worksheet 3 – Self Care Worksheet 120
    1.4 Worksheet 4 – Nutrition Worksheet 124
    1.5 Worksheet 5 – Exercise Worksheet 129
    1.6 Worksheet 6 – Consistency: Practice Makes Better 134

About the Author, Jodi Watkins 137

Acknowledgements

- First of all, I have to thank the Lord, the only Father I have ever had. I ran from you for many years, but I am no longer running. I am allowing You to guide me in everything I do – in life AND in business. You have been here for me just waiting patiently for me to come around. You have pulled me through turmoil and allowed, what I thought was a waste, come together in what I am doing now – serving others as You purposed for me.

I am eternally grateful that you kept me here on this earth to help others in a way that allows them to live a stress-free and healthier lifestyle. At age 41, I finally realized who was truly responsible for anything in my life and that is you, not me. You have given me the strength to write this book and an accountability partner, who forced me to finish what I started. She had no idea, but she was helping me grow just as much as I was helping her, by providing the tools she can now use and make her own in order to gain success in all areas of her life. I started this book without you, Lord, but I am finishing it in your grace. You pulled me out of the wilderness and gave me the eyes to see more for myself.

"Your word is a lamp for my feet, a light on my path."
- Psalms 119:105

I want to thank each and every person who had a part in my upbringing, in keeping me focused when the world around me seemed to be crumbling, who believed in me when I didn't have it in me to keep going. God put you all in my life for a reason. I am truly appreciative and I acknowledge you.

- To those individuals specifically who raised and influenced me in Fernandina Beach, FL, my hometown of 18 years. Many of you were trying to show me a better life, some of you were learning lessons right along with me – both good and bad. While the world around us was cold, there was some warmth with knowing we all had each other. I appreciate you more than you know.

- I had more guardians than I knew what to do with and that was how you kept me safe – My grandparents, my mom, and my Aunt "Viv" (you took me in when I had no place to go), who are all in heaven watching down on us. My Godparents, who were rightly appointed by my mom and who have truly stepped up in her absence. I could easily write a separate book about each person who helped me push through when times were rough and push forward when I felt like nothing was left. This book is the first of many that will become available as the Lord provides me with the words. I just want you to know that I appreciate you all so much. You were brought into my life as earth angels – mentors – friends. You helped me get through a time where life didn't seem to be worth living. I am truly grateful.

- To my brothers and sisters who weren't blood family, but who were family nonetheless. You were there for me just like we should be as family. To my actual sister, Morgan Kaye, who did not get to see this earth but as an angel, but who is keeping our mother company in Heaven and who has been watching over me since I was seven years old. To my crew in high school who got me into trouble, but also kept me in school. You guys did not let me quit and I can't thank you enough for that. You know who you are. We had our ring leader and then we had each other. Many of you are no longer on this earth. Some of you have gone to be with our Father and I pray you were able to get to know Him before you left this earth. Just know you are truly missed and thought about every day. For those of you who have gone down a path that seems dark, just know your circumstances CAN change. All you have to do is submit and allow God into your life. He WILL take over and He WILL give you the life He wants you to live.

- To Ms. Wallace, of Wallace-Pierson Travel in Fernandina Beach: Thank you for making it possible for me to attend Senior Night. I wouldn't have been able to go without you. I am truly grateful we are still in touch and for your continued support.

- To Mrs. Mattie Yokley, I will never forget you - my mentor, basketball, and track coach. You made sure I made it to basketball games and track meets. You looked out for us kids who needed someone like you in our lives. You made sure I had basketball shoes and taught me the meaning of working hard. I did not know how much of an impact you would have on me, but I want you to know that you helped mold me into the person I am today. The person who refuses to quit. While it took me a really long time to finally get to where I needed to be mentally in order to walk my path, I wouldn't change any of it or any of the people who came into my life.

- To my "big sister," who STILL looks out for me to this day, even though you have a family of your own. You know who you are without being named. You have never let me suffer and I can't thank you enough for that. You taught me a whole lot about life, and we are both living proof that diligence trumps mistakes. Our upbringing set us up for failure, but we refused to accept that later down the road. Failure is NOT an option. You are doing amazing things in your own life and WE have moved past anything that could have torn us apart. WE are not going to let what we didn't have define us. WE are going to make sure we give more to our own families and use our past as a motivator for what we don't want in life. God has given us both an awakening in our lives that will never be taken for granted or taken away by any human. He raised us up through the mess and gave us the opportunities to change the story in a way we never could have imagined when we were younger. Our trials are now our tribulations. Our journey is our reward. We are living lives He always knew we could live.

- To my husband, who I don't deserve. We have been through it. You have YET to give up on me. I have put you through more than you ever should have been put through due to my own insecurities and internal struggles. I spent years dwelling on my past instead of reaching for the future. I didn't appreciate you, and I apologize for that. I am thankful for you and glad you are still here with me, supporting me, and being an amazing daddy to our little girl. I don't know where my life would be had we not found each other. I do know that I couldn't imagine it differently.

- To my daughter (shown on the cover and filled with life), who inspires me and motivates me more than you will ever know. Being your mom helped me come out of my comfort zone, challenge myself, write this book, be transparent and simply, appreciate life. Little girl, you are my world. You are the reason I breathe. You are the reason I work so hard. You are my why. You simply being you is why I have found myself. You are writing books and wanting to help other children, even though you are a child yourself. You have this amazing spirit about you. I love you every day and I also love the person you have and will become. Thank you for always giving me a reason to wake up in the mornings and keep crushing my goals. You are amazing. Never stop being you – creative and funny, not worrying about what the outside world thinks, and challenging yourself. The Lord truly blessed me when He placed you inside me. He gave me a second chance. He gave me … You.

- To Community Life Ministry (CLM), who have become family to my family and supports me and continues to allow me to grow through Christ

- I also want to thank my good friend, Jamie Johnson, who I've known since our days in Fernandina Beach, for contributing her amazing story of consistency to this book. I continue to pray for her and ask that you do the same, for she is blessed beyond belief and also found comfort in the Lord this past year as she battles PTSD, which should be called PTSI – it's not a disorder, but an injury. In time, it CAN be healed.

- If you would ever like to share your story, I would love to hear from you. There will be more books to follow and much more on the horizon. As God is my witness, I am taking everyone on this journey with me who wants to be here. I appreciate you all and I look forward to continuing the journey God currently has placed before me. See Jamie's story in the "Consistency" chapter of this book.

Preface

My true health journey began with the loss of the person I knew all my life – my mom. While we didn't have the best relationship for many years, she definitely taught me a lot about life, mostly what NOT to do, but that is perfectly fine. All the lessons made me the person I am today. I wouldn't change any of it now. I am now learning to cope and using what I have seen in my past to help others deal with their pain in hopes they don't have to endure it for as long as I did. I forgive my mom, I forgive myself, and we are made to always forgive those who forsake us. This is what I have done in my life now and will continue to do from this day forward. The Lord will bring us through the mud if we allow Him to. All I had to do was submit.

Dedicated to **Diane Lynn Van Hoose (Knott)** 2/2/50-9/29/09

Dear Lord, You have taken me down this journey I know as my life and have allowed me to use everything in it to help others in their journeys as well. I am truly grateful You never gave up on me. You forgave me for my sins as Your son paid the ultimate price for us humans. You have provided me with these gifts that I never knew were there, but You always did. You have allowed me to give everything I have learned and sew into others what you have sewn into me. Lord, I just ask that everyone who reads this book, reads with an open mind and willingness to know what I did not know for so long – it is not up to us to control everything in our lives. It is up to us to learn how to grow through You and adopt a mindset that will allow us to gain understanding in areas in our lives we may never have understood before.

Lord, I ask that you provide and bless each person reading this book and give them the insight you have given me. Father, you are the only Father, and without you, we are nothing. You are forever King. You have taken me out of the darkness, where I was once lost, and have become the forever light at my feet when I take a step out. You tell me to go and I just go now. I no longer worry about where I am going or where you are taking me. I just go. I am truly grateful you have placed the gift of writing within me. You have taken what I once used as a way to release and have allowed me to use it in a more powerful way, to share with others what You have shown me. Thank you, Lord. You are our Savior. You are our provider. As long as we are with You, we are without nothing. You provide everything we need and I am truly humbled by what you have provided me – the gift of truly living. In Your precious son's name, Amen.

Dear reader, thank you again for your support and love. God bless you!

Read on. For the Lord our God told me the following in writing this book and sharing the information with you:

> *"This will bring health to your body and nourishment to your bones"*
>
> –Proverbs 3:8

Introduction

**Why Are You Here?
Live the Life You've Always Dreamed!**

"Let the peace of Christ rule in your hearts, since as members of one body you were called to peace. And be thankful. Let the message of Christ dwell among you richly as you teach and admonish one another as you teach and admonish one another with all wisdom through psalms, hymns, and songs from the Spirit, singing to God in your hearts."

– Colossians 3:15-16

This book encompasses the journey and steps that have been truly helpful in my own life. I pray you will read this so you can reach total health and fulfillment in your own lives. Read it carefully, but put into *practice* the insight that was given to me to share through years of a constant process. I hope this will get you to stop wasting money on "get skinny quick" fads and allow you to understand and begin to use science-backed principles to achieve everything you *desire*. Know that everything I wrote in this book comes from the heart – they are words given through journey that never made sense to me up until this past year. The Lord has brought me through, and He will do the same for you if you allow Him to. He provided me with the curiosity that allowed me to alleviate all the confusion in my own journey by getting educated and believing in the *possibilities*. Through experience, I've made it a consistent practice in my life. I pray you will do the same. Each day is a journey, but if you are willing to become aware of things in your life that are holding you back, you may be amazed at what and how much you can accomplish.

Do I know everything? Not at all. Nevertheless, I have been chosen to give everything that I have picked up over the years. I have the desire to continue walking in this path so that I will continue to learn and provide more to those who rely on me. The great thing about human sciences is that new data gets released every day. The not so good thing is there are so many people out there who are telling you how to live your life, it can pull you into another direction. This is where research comes into play and knowing what to look for and what is not the best information. The Lord has guided me to the right people in my own journey. I constantly research and rely on Him to ensure I am using the best and latest in science to help those who yearning for a healthier life. I am still using the tactics and knowledge I have been given and will for the rest of my life. Consistency is key. Patience and persistence are vital. You didn't become unhealthy in thirty days and you won't achieve total health in thirty days. It worries me when people brag about losing 70+ pounds in one month. Not only is this not healthy and is internally damaging if not done correctly, but it also normally causes a dip in metabolism and is not something that can or will last. This is why many people get discouraged when it comes to their health journeys and quit.

Nevertheless, if you are willing to put one foot in front of the other and become more patient, you may just find that achieving a life of total health is not as hard as you once thought it to be. Change your habits little by little, change your life. The choice is yours. You can continue to be miserable or you can take ownership and be willing to change. You can achieve literally anything you put your mind to if you want it badly enough. Wanting it a little bit isn't going to get you anywhere. You have to REALLY want it. You have to wake up each day smiling, knowing God has placed you in total control of your thoughts and choices, whether you are ready to believe that or not.

Through my own journey and the mentorship I provided to others over the years, the Lord has equipped me with a six-step process that can and will change your life forever. But you must be open to the possibility that you can live this life without misery or frustration. It takes constant effort to make necessary changes. Reading this book will not change you. However, if you read this and *put it into practice*, you will realize a healthy lifestyle is feasible. Wishing it will NOT make it so. DOING the work is what produces change and growth.

This process will not work for you if you would rather find the magic pill that does not exist. This is not for you if you would rather continue wasting money on the latest fads just to lose the progress you made once you get tired of that method. This is not a 30-day fix or 100-day challenge. This is your *life*. Those are great to help you get started, but how you finish is the important part. It's great to start, but you also must enjoy it and embrace it to want to continue. This process is for those who are ready to step out and achieve total health through *proven* methods and the Spirit that is working through me to give you this information.

This system has not only changed my life, but it has also changed the lives of those who have allowed me to be their guide. It also changed my family dynamic. Now that I am in a better place, I am able to approach situations differently in my family. I am not nearly as reactive as I used to be. I am more open to the fact I cannot change anyone else. All I could do was focus on changing me and allowing my walk to be the mentorship others need. When it comes to health, I am blessed to have a child who is active and healthy. My husband was able to come off his blood pressure medication and get more quality sleep at night through regular exercise and paying more attention to what he was putting into his body. When you read this book, I ask that you share it with your friends and family. Allow them to see how God is working in your life and how you have developed into the person you always wanted to be. They will begin to ask questions. I pray you will tell them all about your journey so they will also be inspired to live a healthier lifestyle. This should be contagious and I never want you to hold it in. Share it with others. Help them become better versions of themselves. Let's build a community together.

What really changed everything for me mentally was my willingness to finally open up to the spiritual aspect of things. Due to my internal pride and habitual nature, it took a true act of God to finally get me to say, "Enough is enough" and stop trying to control every situation. I was to a point where it seemed everything in my life was going down the drain. I wasn't able to unleash the gifts God gave me. I was limiting myself. I finally had to do what the famous quote says – "Let go and let God." Once I did that, doors began to open, the people I met were of a different energy, and my life truly changed for the better. If you have not learned to allow the Spirit to be inside of you, that may be the first thing you look into. Once you have done that, you may find you want to be led in a way you've never been led before. You will be more open to using the tools in this book and you will want to learn more about yourself.

Let's talk about the system God has given me to share with you.

What is the system?

STEP ONE: Mindset Shift.

In order to truly receive the gifts of God, we have to stop blaming others, take ownership in our flaws (turn the mirror around), stop dwelling on the past, and believe in ourselves. We must truly believe that we CAN achieve *anything* as long as we put forth the effort.

STEP TWO: Time Management.

Establishing a good routine is so important in our daily lives. I divulge how schedules can help you "find more time in your day" just by becoming more accountable. You'll do a time audit and you may find that what you thought you didn't have time for, maybe just wasn't a priority in your life.

STEP THREE: Self-Care and Positivity.

Let's focus on self-care and positivity. If you don't love yourself, how can you expect anyone else to love you? You will literally sabotage anything good in your life because internally, you don't feel worthy. I did it for years unintentionally.

STEP FOUR: Nutrition

Science is always your best bet when it comes to nutrition. Time is your most valuable asset. Stop wasting it on temporary fad diets that don't teach you anything! It's time to wake up and do the work! INVEST in your health and be willing to put some effort into this portion of the process.

STEP FIVE: Exercise

You don't necessarily need a gym to get a good workout. Hiring someone who has experience with your needs is a great way to get started the right way and not get frustrated or more importantly, injured. It doesn't take a whole lot. It just takes you wanting to start and having a goal so you continue. The key to overall success is all in step six: consistency and practice. If you want to become better at something, you must repeat it over and over. This is called practicing. Reaching goals takes consistency, letting go of any pride that may get in the way, and being open to learning new ideas. Otherwise, goals become dreams. The journey does NOT stop once you reach your first goal. You have to continue setting goals so you have incentive to keep going. Once you reach a certain point in your journey, you should WANT to continue because you have come so far and are *no longer* looking back. By this time, you have most likely empowered so many others to begin their journeys that you'll want to learn even more. It will be a *desire*. This is where the *lifestyle* begins.

The Lord has empowered me to find true health and happiness by developing the new habits that led me to the goal and have an agenda that has allowed me to be more successful in my own life. I had to stop wanting more and operating out of lack. I had to become more appreciative of what I already had (which is a lot more than many people).

Now, I use my desires as a way to self-reflect. I pray about them and know that if they are meant to happen, they will. Without a mindset shift, literally nothing will begin to change in our lives. We all have to go through this. It is so important to focus on getting your mind right before we even dabble in the world of food diaries and customized workout programs. Otherwise, it all becomes a more complicated set of instructions than it needs to be and you will quit.

Without the proper mindset that allows for prosperity and growth, the root of the problem will not surface. Through examining ourselves, we may just find that we are holding ourselves back from all things great. For instance, through self-reflection, I learned I was very confident, yet lacked self-esteem. This held me back tremendously. It will take a *breakthrough* for goals to be accomplished. Put the information in this book to use and you may just find that everything you need to get where you want to be is inside the person you see in the mirror. If you have not done so already, ask the Lord to guide you as you read this book. Ask Him to be the leader in your heart. Ask Him if this is the right process for you and to help you use these tools as you are meant to use them in your own life.

Start today and learn the steps, keep a journal and answer the questions in this book. Do the worksheets at the end. Then see how your life changes for the positive over time. Will it happen overnight? Of course not! But did the root of the problem happen in one day? Not at all. It took you years to learn how to be stressed and overwhelmed and develop habits that do NOT provide a path towards your health and wellness goals. Now it's going to take some time to undo all that.

I can attest from experience, it is well worth the wait and the work. I would rather get my you know what together in my 40's than never – ending up on my death bed with tons of regrets – wouldn't you? Hopefully you're younger than me when you read this book and can work on your limiting beliefs even sooner than I have, but maybe you're my age or older. Age does not matter. If you are doing it, *that is all that matters!*

Research has shown that most people do not reach their full potential until after the age of 40. Most of us have to go through the mud before we open our hearts to allow the Lord to guide us. This is what allows us to have a story to tell. We are broken, but we are *gracefully broken* in order to take on the journey and be vulnerable. The key is being willing to make some key internal changes. If you are not willing to change and take steps that will allow you to become a better overall version of yourself, don't expect anything in your life to change for the better – that includes your health.

Chapter 1
Mindset Development

Be kind and compassionate to one another, forgiving each other, just as in Christ God forgave you.

- Ephesians 4:32

1.1 Stop Blaming Others

Be free through forgiveness of others and yourself!

When I was a little girl, I learned to suppress and bury everything. My childhood was *not* pretty, to say the least. The home wasn't just broken; it was shattered. I became a person who blamed that situation for everything else in my life even up through my thirties. However, that did not do me justice. That way of thinking was not going to allow me to prosper at all. I realize now that even though I thought I had forgiven, I really had just suppressed it all and acted as if it didn't happen. But it did happen. It was embedded into my subconscious and would surface from time to time without my acknowledgement. I was too proud to admit I was being controlled by my past. *I was in control!* Or so I thought.

As time went by and things continued not to go in my favor, I kept wondering why. Why did I have to witness all the things I witnessed early in my childhood? Why did my dad leave and never resurface? Why did my mom think she could save the men in her life? Why didn't I get a scholarship in college? Why did my mom die? Why did it seem as though every door I worked hard to open closed on me soon after? Why didn't this happen? Why didn't that go to plan? Why did I treat that person like I did? So many thoughts of why. All it did was keep me in a place where I could not grow!

I later found myself regretting leaving the military and not researching my options well enough. I regretted so many things. I had wasted so much time trying to do different things. I blamed myself. I needed to take ownership and move on, but I was allowing the past to dictate my future. The negative thoughts in my mind were holding me back from literally everything. Something I had to learn: shoulda, coulda, or woulda will not get you anywhere. Now is the time to put your vision to the test and do whatever you can to be the best possible version of yourself.

I will not sit here and say I never looked back. For years, living in the past kept me from becoming the person I was meant to be. I had to forgive others, forgive myself, and stop living in the past. I had to stop comparing myself to others. I had to stop scrolling through my news feed. How many of you are vicariously living through other people's social media? How many of you are comparing your current situation to others you see? If this is you, it's time to stop! With that being said, if the comparisons are fueling you in a positive way, so be it. However, if you are allowing comparisons to take you out of your path to success, I highly advise reprogramming your mind so you stop holding yourself back. I hear it all the time: "I used to look like this," or "I used to make this amount of money." I did the same thing and compared my current situation to my past, possibly better, situations. The problem is that when I did that, I began to self-sabotage. It caused me to become a bit depressed.

Now that I have become aware of my own limitations, I let the pain and memories and comparisons propel me. I am no longer living in fear as I was before. I am now aware of my fears so that I can face them. I step out of my comfort zone, and I challenge myself. I am no longer walking in my past. I have forgiven those who have wronged me. Most of all, I have forgiven myself. If you do not forgive yourself, you will never grow.

> *Do not judge, and you will not be judged. Do not condemn, and you will not be condemned. Forgive, and you will be forgiven.*
> (Luke 6:37)

It is not our place to judge anyone else. Most of the time, when we judge those around us, it's because we are not willing to look at ourselves closely. When we condemn others, it's because we don't want to face the wrongs we have done to others. Forgiving ourselves is a very difficult thing to do, especially when we are holding so much inside. The Lord asks us to release. He doesn't want to see us in pain. He wants to see us release that pain and learn to listen to Him. This is what I had to do in my own life, and it has helped me in literally every area of my life.

I write these steps not only to help others but also to help myself and hold myself accountable. When I mentor others, everything I tell them is what I have to do as well. When I give others assignments and things to accomplish in their own lives, I do the same things. We are all on this journey. I am just as human as the next person. I am being led by the Lord to bring the lessons in my life to others in hopes they will be able to achieve mental stability and fulfillment in their lives. The only difference between me and some others is that I have made the choice to not allow my past to control my future anymore. I now allow it to propel me to be the best possible version of myself. I am now led by the Spirit instead of my own mind, which got me in trouble more times than I can count.

What else do I have that allows me to stay motivated? I have a why! Her name is Jasmine. She is my blessing, and she is the reason I refuse to stay in the past. It never did anything for me except hold me back and keep me from learning how to change my future. We stay where we are because we allow ourselves to get comfortable. We would rather stay in our comfort zones than step outside of them.

Today, I am a testament to the fact that everything happens for a reason. I used to get upset when people said that, but it was because I didn't know it was true. I couldn't see the future, so I was propelled by fear of the unknown. You grew up in a broken home? That doesn't mean you have to be broken. You dealt with addiction in your family? That doesn't mean you have to be an addict. You grew up around violence and constant betrayal? That doesn't mean you have to be violent and betray others. You were lost? That's okay. If you never give up and you keep plugging and get through all the turmoil in your life, you will look back and be thankful for all the things you saw and went through, and you will be a stronger and better person for all of it. Have faith you will be found, just as I have been.

Maybe you are in a place where you don't believe in the higher power. Maybe you don't believe in God and His capabilities. I am not trying to tell you what to believe or change your belief system. Only you can do that. What I am doing is simply sharing my journey in hopes it will help you. Maybe you will begin to open up to possibilities as I did.

Through my own mindset shift and renewed beliefs, I was brought back into the light. I am truly thankful for that. I had to gain something I did not possess for a long time: faith. I cannot say enough about this because had it not been for this breakthrough in my own life, many things would not be where they are today. For one, you would not be reading this book. Secondly, I would be working some dead-end job that I hate just to pay the bills. I would not be developing trusting relationships with people around me who want to propel me, rather than pull me back. I would have continued to sabotage my marriage because I did not believe I was worthy of that type of love. Lastly, and probably the worst thing I can think of, I would not be a good role model for my daughter. I would let her down because I would be giving her what I had growing up—no direction.

1.2 Don't Dwell on the Past

Forget the former things; do not dwell on the past.
- Isaiah 43:18

No matter where your past took you before, it doesn't have to be your path now. Find an outlet of some sort. Talk to someone who is equipped to listen and help guide you—talk to God (His ears never close and He doesn't make you go into debt)—write a book, say your fears out loud when no one else is around or when everyone is around. Whatever works best for you. If you believe in God, pray. We all need an outlet.

I have implemented so many more things into my own routine. My entire life is better now because I am no longer blaming others or living in the past. I am living life. I was put on this earth to make an impact on the world, and I am now finally doing just that. You were put here for the same reason. Don't hold back. Now is your time!

> The same God distributes different kinds of miracles that accomplish different results through each believer's gifts and ministry as he energizes and activates them. Each believer is given continuous revelation by the Holy Spirit to benefit not just himself but all. (1 Corinthians 12:6 TPT)

Think of a gift you possess. Really dig deep. What is that one thing that just comes naturally to you? Write it down here:

_____

Now use the space here to write down why you are not using that gift to its full potential:

Take a moment to reflect. Do you dwell on the past? Do you think about situations that have pained you so much that it keeps you from reaching your full potential or believing in yourself enough to take a leap of faith?

In the bible reading plan, *Release Forgiveness Towards Others and Yourself*, by Eric Celerier[2], it states "when ... memories come back to haunt us, we need to forgive ... actually, forgive again. This forgiveness is a choice ..."

Here's the thing – if we are constantly reliving the same scenarios that kept us from stepping into our true selves, we will never heal. Those same scenarios will continue to hold us back. In order to get past all the pain we have endured in a past life (going back to point 1.1 – Stop Blaming Others), we have to learn how to forgive as many times as we need to. Not only are we constantly forgiving others for past wrongdoings, but we must also continue to forgive ourselves.

> *"Then Peter came to Jesus and asked, 'Lord, how many times shall I forgive my brother or sister who sins against me? Up to seven times?' Jesus answered, 'I tell you, not seven times, but seventy-seven times"*
>
> – Matthew 18:21-22

Your biggest ally in this journey will be awareness. Learning to be aware of yourself and how you react is how you begin the next portion of mindset development – taking ownership.

1.3 Take Ownership

> *"You will plant but not harvest; you will press olives but not use the oil, you will crush grapes but not drink the wine."*
>
> – Micah 6:15

What does this verse mean to you? Take a moment to think about it.

Have you ever wondered how it has come to pass that you work so hard for something, but the door closed without warning? Was that the path you were meant to take? If the door closed, it was not the correct path for you.

Let's explore this a little more.

Are you currently being led by love or fear? Think about it.

One of the most important parts of step one, and the most difficult for people (including me), is believing in yourself. Fear has taken me from my true potential and allowed me to just be mediocre for so long. It made me doubt my abilities and what I had to offer as a person.

While others believe in me now, up until very recently, I still doubted myself. Instead of thinking about all the things I HAVE accomplished, I would find myself thinking about and dwelling on the things I had not accomplished. Why do we do this to ourselves?

Research shows that people who come from a broken home or who had a parent leave at one point in their life (especially if both occurred) tend to constantly seek approval from the outside world.

In a study about children who are exposed to domestic violence (which I was most of my childhood and into my teen years until I left home), "Children and youth who are exposed to domestic violence experience emotional, mental, and social damage that can affect their developmental growth. Some children lose the ability to feel empathy for others. Others feel socially isolated, unable to make friends as easily due to social discomfort or confusion over what is acceptable"[3]

What happens when the situations around you become toxic? Are you able to recognize this quickly or are you so consumed in trying to please them and gain acceptance that you are blinded by the reality of what is happening?

I believe that we allow ourselves to invite toxic people into our lives so that we can subconsciously replay the scenarios we grew up with. We seek pleasure and happiness through others, instead of first reaching inside ourselves.

Not only is this detrimental to our personal growth, but it can also destroy any great relationship we may have somehow developed, and can lead to constant self-sabotage. If we are used to not receiving true fulfillment in our lives, we will revert back to where we are comfortable. An author named Dodinsky once said: "You have to love yourself because no amount of love from others is sufficient to fill the yearning that your soul requires from you."

What does this quote mean to you? Does it speak to you? Take a moment to really ponder the quote and use the space below to journal your thoughts in order to make them real. If nothing comes to you, seek God for assistance. Learn to "hear" from Him. Allow Him to give you direction on this quote and then continue.

It's time to write a new story. How do you begin to rewrite your story? First, you have to be willing to believe you are worthy of the great things in life. This is the most difficult part because believing in ourselves is NOT normal. This is especially true if you were brought up by someone who did not tell you that you were deserving and loved on a regular basis. Society also writes our story for us if we let it. Negativity can truly hold us back from anything great in life.

I wondered why things weren't working out for me, but it was because deep down, I was not allowing myself to be happy. I was so used to things not working out for me that I actually pulled that negative energy more towards me. All these years it was a vicious cycle.

Think about some things you may have worked toward in your life. How did those things work out for you? Were you doing those things because you felt you were doing good towards others or was it more for monetary gain and social acceptance? Think about it … what were your true intentions?

For me, I can remember being in school and being made fun of because I was wearing hand-me-down clothes. My mom and her husband were addicts, so I just felt very lost and afraid of what my true potential was. That was embedded in me at an early age. While I can no longer blame any of this on the life I have now, I can say that it set the stage for the years to come.

I was so lost during college and even pretty much my entire 15-year military career. I was decent at what I did, but I knew it wasn't what

I wanted to do my entire life. When my mom passed away and I had a child, you would think I could have found some direction. In all actuality, I became more lost. I entered a program I thought I was meant to be in, but looking back, I did that for social acceptance and monetary gain. I did it for a title I thought I needed in order to be more prestigious in the world.

It did not take long for reality to set in and for that program to become a fond memory. It devastated me when things fell apart at that time because I had worked so hard. However, I worked really hard on it for all the wrong reasons. I told myself I was doing it to serve others, but in reality, I was doing it more to serve me. Being relieved from that program took an even bigger toll on my confidence.

As the years went by, I felt like I just went deeper and deeper into a hole that I could not get out of. I began to think that everyone was against me. In reality, I was against me. Therefore, I would never get out of the rut because I was not allowing myself to move forward. I kept going back to that child who was so involved in trying to gain acceptance that she became lost in her own mind with no true direction or path to take.

It wasn't until the past year or so that I finally decided enough was enough. There are so many people out here doing great things that don't know half of what I know and are leading others down a path that won't allow them to be truly successful. I wanted to be able to influence these people on a broader spectrum, share my story, and hopefully impact them in a positive way. But how? Again, I had no direction. I was doing tons of research and helping others daily, but I still lacked the confidence to take it further.

I've always enjoyed writing, so it just seemed natural to use that strength to get my ideas out so that hopefully the script will be a way to help others along their journeys and keep them from enduring the same pain I endured for all these years, mostly without even realizing it.

My journey now is not perfect. Yours won't be either. No person's journey is linear. WE are not perfect beings. We simply must aim for progress.

There will be bumps in the road, life WILL happen, and you WILL have to pick yourself up during these times ... make sure you pick yourself up. There are still many days where self-doubt and lack of confidence – fear of the unknown – surface within me.

The difference now is that I can identify it before it takes me down a path of self-destruction. I am clearer on what I want to do. While I still don't have an exact plan of how to do it, I am working on it. Whether your journey is in life, a goal, getting healthier, making better choices, no matter what it is, the journey is never linear. There will be times you are afraid and want to quit. There will be times you enter a room, all eyes on you, and you want to turn back around. There will be fear. There will be doubt. The way you overcome that is to continue taking steps in a forward direction. Don't turn around. Walk into that room with your head held high. You have made it. You are here. You are doing what you were put here to do.

Make it your priority to be your biggest fan even if no one else supports you. Maybe you feel as though you walk in the room and no one knows you. Maybe they don't. But you know you. That's all that matters. They WILL know you because you were put here to be known and to have an impact on others.

I am truly grateful for those who have supported me through my venture. Not everyone has, of course. There have been some who didn't think I had it in me. Nevertheless, many who know me and have come to know me, have made it possible for me to get over my own self-doubt and keep pursuing what I am truly meant to do – help as many people as possible. Maybe you didn't have a rough upbringing, but other things in your life have happened that have made you not want to try again. Whatever you do, don't be like that. Do not let other things dictate what you do or don't do.

Listen to your heart. If you know in your heart you were put on this earth to make an impact, do whatever it takes to make that impact. Believe in yourself. Be your biggest fan. That way, when no one else believes in you, you still keep moving forward in the direction that will take you further than you have ever been before. Don't worry about what the rest of the world is doing. If you want to help people, help them. Find people who will guide you on your journey. People who have done it themselves. Listen to those people. Don't listen to the people who don't want you to succeed. Listen to those who do. Listen to YOU.

How do you reprogram your subconscious mind after years of writing old stories over and over? Let's take a formula from a very well-known book that I highly recommend. Read on and use the information to begin the process.

I began using this formula soon after reading it. I highly recommend trying it for yourself. You may get surprised as to where you are able to go from here. It is called the "Self-Confidence Formula" and can be found in the book, *Think and Grow Rich*, by Napoleon Hill.

Here is a little bit of what you will find as you go through this formula. I highly recommend this book as part of your reading list.

"The Self-Confidence Formula (abridged):

1. I know that I have the ability to achieve the object of my Definite Purpose in life.

2. I realize the dominating thoughts of my mind will eventually reproduce themselves in an outward, physical action and gradually transform themselves into physical reality.

3. I know through the principle of autosuggestion that any desire I persistently hold in my mind will eventually seek expression through some practical means of attaining the object.

4. I have clearly written down a description of my *Definite Chief Aim* in life. I will never stop trying until I developed sufficient self-confidence for its attainment.

5. I fully realize that no wealth or position can long endure unless built upon truth and justice." [6]

Why is all of this so important? Well, it's simple really. In order to change your situation, you have to believe you are worthy of change. You will not succeed in anything you do until you truly believe you are someone who deserves what you are working for. This goes for anything, whether it be health and wellness, your career, and basically any situation you come across in life. You will not achieve what you dream until you give yourself a pass and allow yourself to understand that you are still here for a reason. You are here to change the world. You are 100% deserving of everything good in life. Getting to this point may require saying and believing things to and for yourself until you allow yourself to accept who you are and the impact you were placed on this earth to have. None of us were put here by chance. There is a plan for each of us.

1.4 Believe in Yourself ... You CAN DO THIS!

> *"Do not conform to the pattern of this world, but be transformed by the renewing of your mind. Then you will be able to test and approve what God's will is – his good, pleasing and perfect will.*
> – Romans 12:2

The beliefs you have of yourself is where it begins – a renewal of the mind. These beliefs are called affirmations. The infamous Tony Robbins puts emphasis on another ritual called "incantations." So, what is the difference between the two?

What are affirmations and why use them? Affirmations "are spoken words of encouragement." Incantations, on the other hand, "are about embodying the meaning *behind* the words, which is why they are so powerful. With incantations, not only are you speaking words of empowerment, you are using your body and your voice."[9] This makes it more of a reality.

So how can you come up with your own affirmations?

First, what is a negative thought that you feel about yourself? One example of this would be, "I am not worthy of anything good." Another example that I hear a lot when I talk to people is, "I hate the way I look." The first example is one that I had to overcome myself.

Second, you need to write it down. Now get rid of this thought by tearing, burning, or shredding the piece of paper you just wrote that thought on. (See mine and Elsie's video at https://youtu.be/fKolmL7mGmU).

Lastly, you need to write down the complete opposite of what you wrote before. The opposite of that negative thought is the center of your first affirmation. For example, "I am worthy of ALL things good" or simply #3 on my list: "I am worthy."[11]

Have your affirmations hanging up where you will see them each morning when you wake up and every night before you go to bed. Then use incantations to say them aloud, moving around and even yelling them if you have to! I don't care how silly or stupid you feel! The point of this is to retrain your subconscious mind so that you will allow yourself to succeed without fear and without sabotaging yourself unintentionally. I often tell people to "become comfortable feeling uncomfortable." That is the gateway to change. If we want to change, we must take risks. We have to become uncomfortable. It is scary. It is not easy. However, it is amazing to become transformed more and more each day as you progress. I am a true testimony.

As my spiritual journey became stronger, I relied on verses to get me through the day. The verse that I kept everywhere and looked at mostly was Psalms 139:14, *"I praise you because I am fearfully and wonderfully made; your works are wonderful. I know that full well."*

I really like the Passion Translation of this verse. It says, *"I thank you, God, for making me so mysteriously complex! Everything you do is marvelously breathtaking, it simply amazes me to think about it! How thoroughly you know me, Lord!"*

He knew me before I knew me. The reason I went through all the trials in my life was so that He could bring me where I am today. I am able to share all this with you because of what I have seen in my life. None of it was my fault. I just wasn't being led by the right person. I was being led by people instead of the Lord. In knowing that now, I have been able to do so much work on me from the inside out and can now help others do the same. This is the book that needed to be written, the way it needed to be written. This is the story that can now be shared.

In order to get through the chaos in your mind and the negative thoughts, you will want to dig deep with this because learning to love yourself is the first step in truly changing your life and allowing yourself to be successful in virtually anything you do. I have and will continue to take these steps for as long as I am willing.

Remember, just like anything else, once you have made a breakthrough, you must continue the process. Saying the affirmations out loud for one or two days is not going to make it true. It is NOT going to change the limiting beliefs you currently have about yourself. You need to speak these new truths until your subconscious mind takes over and allows you to truly BELIEVE what you are saying.

Here is my list of daily affirmations. You may use what I have written here or come up with your own in the space provided. Regardless of what you choose, you must remember that it requires you to make the effort to change. Saying you want something doesn't matter until you put forth the action to make the changes.

Jodi's Daily Affirmations/Incantations:

I love myself
I am beautiful
I am worthy
I DESERVE all great things in life
I attract people who KNOW I am valuable to their lives
I am the expert in my field and willingly exemplify integrity and discipline
I am a survivor
I bring about positive change
I am amazing
I BELIEVE in myself and my capabilities
I do not allow the world to bring me down

I have divine intervention leading me on my path
I conquer all challenges
I get out of my comfort zone each day
I make an impact each day
I AM persistent
I DO NOT QUIT!

If you are having trouble coming up with affirmations for yourself, let's go back and use the tools above to help.

First, choose a negative thought you have about yourself and externalize it by writing it down here:

_____

Once you have done that, think of the opposite and write that down. This is the time to let go of that negative thought and focus only on the positive thought. Therefore, take out a new sheet of paper and write the positive thought down there. This is how you begin writing your new story.

_____

Use this space to come up with 5-10 affirmations of your own.

Will there be hard times? Yes. Will there be situations that challenge you in every way possible? Yes. If you are in the mindset that you are not deserving, you will never be able to see the positive in any situation. You will encounter others and will never impact their lives in a positive way because you are too much in your own head. You will attract the energy you give out. Therefore, if you are constantly miserable and worrying, you will attract others who will pull you down even more. This is NOT acceptable in your life!

Repeat after me: "I REFUSE to accept negativity in my life." From here on out, live by those words. Reach out to God when times are hard. Get in the Word. You will find all your answers there. I know I have so far. Continue putting God first in your life and allowing Him to lead you. Doors that once were closed may begin to open. The door you are meant to go into will surely open. All you have to do is be obedient and have Faith. According to Dr. Stephanie L. Foster, the three basic steps in developing Faith That Delivers are: "Believe, Receive, and Act." You can NOT change unless you are willing to act on the ideas and thoughts driven by the Holy Spirit. It does you no good to hear the word. You must be *"doers of the word"* (James 1:22).

You worry about what others think of you. You worry about what you say and what you do. You want to fit it. Can you relate to these statements? They described who I was for the better part of my life. It wasn't until I finally released myself from my own bondage that I was able to view the world in an entirely different way and impact lives in a whole new way.

Our limitations are programmed by our own subconscious mind. We dictate our own outcome. We have the ultimate decision to make: are we going to allow ourselves to be buried under the past and things we are unable to control? Or are we going to free ourselves and allow ourselves to experience a happier, more fulfilled life? Our happiness does not come from the outside world.

You will never be happy and fulfilled if you are constantly living in fear, scarcity, and doubt. Keep this in mind as you continue your day.

If you want to change, you have to get outside of your comfort zone in your own head first and foremost.

Otherwise, you will say you want a different life, but your habits and rituals that got you where you are will continue to hold you back. You will always go back to your comfort zone and revert to self-sabotage until you make it a point each and every day to deliberately take yourself OUT of your comfort zone.

You will have to develop new rituals and habits strategically in order to progress. Will you fail from time to time? Of course. These failures you endure are there to hold you back. They are there to push you to be the greatest version of yourself over time. You just have to make the effort to change. If you are not willing to do that, you might as well close this book now and go back to where you were – never fulfilling your true potential in life and staying where you are and where you are comfortable.

If you are ready for a change, continue. Implement what you read through the guidance I have been provided and the journey I have been on. Take massive action, and see the rewards you receive as you continue this for the rest of your life. The journey is nonstop and will challenge you in every possible way.

How will you overcome the challenges? Will you shut down and hope it gets better, or will you push through and continue working for what you desire? You have to allow yourself to get there. You have to say things to yourself that will make you want it and do what it takes to get there. You have to believe in yourself and know you are capable of so many amazing things. This is the first step in total health. Once you have done this, the possibilities are endless.

For years, actually up until recently, I was limiting myself. I don't know why. Not believing in myself never made me feel better. It just made me sad, frustrated, and feeling unhappy with my situation. I blamed my choices on others, when the decisions were all mine. I blamed others for what was happening in my life. While these things may have impacted my earlier thinking, it should not have remained an excuse later on in life. But it did – and things continued to happen that kept me in this negative state to where I just kept blaming the world for what was happening to me.

This quote stood out to me as I was learning about letting go:

> "You can't feed today's hunger with yesterday's meal"
> – TJ Milam

This is so true! How many times have you thought about changing your ways or doing something amazing, but then your fear and your memories of your past and the things you did not accomplish crept into your thoughts and held you back? Failure makes you stop. If you let it, it will keep you from pursuing your goal. We have all been there I'm sure. I used to dwell on so many things. It took me so long to realize that everything I thought was happening TO me was actually happening FOR me. I also had to realize the failures were actually pushing me to where I truly needed to be. However, we do not see what is right in front of us when our plans are not being carried out as we hoped.

When physician assistant school didn't work out (the program I entered for a title and acceptance and what I was working toward when my mom passed away), I blamed the Air Force. However, it wasn't their fault. I wasn't focused. I didn't put my all into it. I was still mourning the loss of my mom, who passed away while I was taking my prerequisite finals for the program. While, in my mind, I wanted to change the healthcare system by being in it, all the wrong reasons came to the forefront and became more important than my beginning driver: monetary gain, social acceptance, and to avenge the death of my mom which came out of hospital negligence. I was depressed for a while, but my coping mechanism was to bury it all. I just buried it and moved on to the next. I slapped a band-aid on it because that is what I was good at doing – covering it up and continuing on. I wrote a poem about it, but I never shared until a couple years later at an open mic night during NCO (Non-Commissioned Officer) Academy in 2012. I thought the wound was healed, but it wasn't. I called it the dagger in my heart. It led me into a dark corner, but I couldn't completely shut down or mope around. I still had obligations and had to continue on the flight line. I was also working on my master's degree at the time and began taking prerequisites to apply for nursing programs. That was my way to keep going. Suppression does not create healing, it just creates a standard in your life where you bury things and think they will go away. Nursing school didn't work out either. So, what did I do next? I went to the Air Force Reserve recruiter and found another way. That didn't work out either.

What I didn't know at that time was that I was holding myself back from greater things. I thought it had to be one way. I had to constantly feel like I was working towards something that would give me status in this world. I craved *success*! That's all I could think about. I wasn't thinking about the journey. I wasn't thinking about how I would get there. I wanted a title on my name. I wanted to *belong*. I wanted to feel achieved. Have you ever felt this way? Have you ever allowed these feelings of wanting to fit in somewhere to absolutely control you? This is where I was. The sad part is I did not even realize what I was doing.

The problem is, subconsciously, I didn't truly BELIEVE any of those things were going to work out for me because I had been let down most of my life.

This is the time you must sit down and evaluate yourself.

What in your life has held you back from your true potential? Go ahead and write it down here. Think of 5-6 things in your life you can think of that happened in your childhood that is still resonating in your mind today:

Now that you've written these things down, <u>*let them go*</u>. Stop allowing them to keep you from being the amazing person you were meant to be!

Have you ever seen a poor person walking down the street? Do they look happy or do they look like they've let life beat them to a pulp? Have you ever thought to ask why they are in the situation they're in?

If you do ask them, are you present? Do you truly *listen* to their story? Is it different from yours or is it they just allowed situations that were out of their control get them to a point where they just gave up? Listen and take notice.

Are you willing to allow yourself to get to that point? What do you want out of life?

What do you TRULY want? What are your *desires*?

Answer here:

_____

Being willing to examine yourself is a frightening adventure, believe me. However, it is one I highly advise anyone going on who may be in the same boat I was in before my journey began. As I said before, it won't be easy. Nevertheless, the most fulfilling things in life aren't easy. They are, however, *worth it.*

When you feel like you can't keep going, remember these words that I wrote back in 2017. You CAN ALWAYS get passed the present. It may seem dark at the time, but it just means the light is going to shine a lot brighter on you when you come out of it all.

"I will rise up
I will not be defeated
I will rise up
Even when my energy is depleted
There's no stopping me now
I'm on my way

Yesterday has passed
I can only focus on today
Failure is a mindset
It's only temporary
Success comes from wisdom
No one progresses from being stationary"

On my side, I have the following words tattooed by the great artist, Tito Zambrano, as a reminder of where I've been and where I plan to go. I wrote it before I went to see him and he did his magic to make it come to life and be something I could be proud of:

"Failure leads to wisdom
Wisdom leads to prosperity
We only live once"

Even though I have always had this wisdom, I did not always use it. You have the wisdom. It's now YOUR turn to use it.

Chapter 2
Time Management

2.1 Wake Up Earlier

> *"Very early in the morning, while it was still dark, Jesus got up, left the house and went off to a solitary place, where he prayed."*
> - Mark 1:35

When it comes to maximizing my time, there are some things that have truly helped me:

- Wake up earlier (start with an extra 10 minutes, then work up as your body gets used to your new schedule)
- Turn off the TV and silence the phones while working on important tasks
- Set a timer, so your brain is fresh when having to perform at a higher level (I set a 20- minute timer for tasks with a 5-10-minute break, where I will do some jumping jacks, stretch, walk around, or just do something different to take my mind off the task for a moment)
- Don't waste time on things that aren't making you better – this includes people (set boundaries)
- Spend time with your passion AND your family

"You wake up at WHAT time?!"

When I tell people what time I normally wake up each day, I get a look like "are you serious?!" Then, there's the infamous, "why?".

I have so many people tell me why they can't wake up earlier. Instead, I wonder if they would consider it if the reason *FOR* waking up earlier far outweighed the reasons against it. Why *CAN'T* you? Can you not physically wake up earlier? Do you have an underlying condition where you physically are unable to wake up earlier? These are the questions I want to ask them back, but I normally just let them continue. They come up with reasons why they *CAN'T* wake up at that time. It's not often I hear someone say, "Well, I *COULD* wake up at that time, I just choose not to."

When they are telling me all the reasons why they *CAN'T* wake up earlier, they are actually just telling themselves why it isn't important enough for them to wake up earlier. They are training their subconscious mind to not allow them to wake up any earlier. Therefore, they won't. They will continue to have goals that never come about. They will continue to stay where they are because they are not willing to do something that they haven't done before – in this case, wake up earlier.

I used to be the same. I used to always say why I couldn't do something. Just as we can use affirmations to help us become more positive, we also can use statements of comfort to help us not feel so bad about choices we make. These statements can also be called, *excuses*.

Before I began waking up earlier and as I would say the same things others say to me now, I never really thought about the fact it just wasn't important enough for me *TO* do it. That is the real truth.

There was a time where I was working all day (12-13 hours) on the flight line, taking three classes (two for nursing and one for my master's degree), AND had my then one-and-a-half-year-old. I already was not getting much sleep, so waking up even earlier seemed crazy. Nevertheless, the only way I could get everything done that I needed to get done BEFORE I went to work was to get up earlier. That is where it began.

When I got out of the military, I began training clients and teaching group classes early in the morning. I wanted to stay on that schedule. It worked for me. That was six years ago.

I do not necessarily *HAVE* to wake up as early as I do most days now. I simply *CHOOSE* to. In order to get tasks done and fulfill my obligations to my family, it's a necessity. What I am doing in life now – being a wife, mom, and self-employed entrepreneur who helps others achieve greatness is more important than anything else I have done in my life. It is the reason I wake up early. It is my motivation. Nevertheless, I never judge anyone for their choices. I have definitely been there.

I remember the days of feeling exhausted everyday (it comes in cycles and the last cycle was actually pretty recent). The days of just not wanting to do anything ... not wanting to *"adult,"* as I call it. We all have those days. I still have them every now and then, though not quite as often as I used to.

The difference now is when I have them, I remember Proverbs 3:5-6 (ERV – Easy to Read Version), *"Trust in the Lord completely, and don't depend on your own knowledge. With every step you take, think about what he wants, and he will help you go the right way. Don't trust in your own wisdom, but fear and respect the Lord and stay away from evil [in this case, laziness]. If you do this, it will be like a refreshing drink and medicine for your body."*

The exhaustion worsened when I didn't like the job I was doing or the people I was around each day. That made getting out of bed even harder, no matter what hours of the day I was working. I worked a job that was 24/7/365. It never stopped. While we would swap out and trade shifts often, it still took its toll. Nevertheless, I did it. Why? Because that's what we were taught. Just do the job and conform. My generation was taught that from an early age. Just suck it up. This is why the military was so easy for me. While I was not too keen on conforming, I was able to just "do the job."

There were no entrepreneurs or women business owners when I was in school. If there were, we surely didn't hear much about them, much less *know* them. We were taught to just work for someone else. The military followed suit very well. "Just shut up and color," is the phrase we all knew, no matter what branch we served.

As I said above, I wasn't much on conforming. I always colored "outside the lines" a little. Sometimes, it was too much for my supervision to handle, but later on, as I got more into supervisory roles, it helped me play a larger role in the success of others and take up for those who deserved it. I was well respected because of the way I began to operate. It got to a point where I stopped making excuses why it *couldn't* be done and began to find ways to *get* it done.

I began to desire more. I wanted to help people on a bigger level. After my mom's death in 2009, I looked at life a lot differently. I was seven months pregnant at the time and that made me really think – if I didn't change my ways and begin challenging myself more, I would continue the cycle of children who don't know the *possibilities* in life. I would not be happy and I would always wonder "what if."

A lot happened after that and up until now, but during the process, I realized that I would wake up earlier when I had to. If I had an important assignment or test to study for that would change the entire outcome of mine and my family's future, I would wake up to work on it or study. At that time, I was getting maybe three hours of sleep each night – but it was worth it – because it was important. I wasn't focusing on my health, I was focusing on the goal at that time – which didn't involve my health. In hindsight, I know now that was not the path I was meant to take. I had to begin learning more about how to take care of my body – internally and externally. Back then, I was not walking with the Lord. Nevertheless, He was guiding me anyway. It just took me a while to recognize it.

The point in all this is that time is the most precious thing we have in life. In order to achieve great things, we sometimes have to be willing to do things that many others aren't willing to do. Just as everything else in this book, the more you do it, the better you get. You may even have your own testimony one day about how you went from being a night owl to a morning person. You may even say to yourself, "self, why did we not do this a long time ago?" We should never dwell on what we have not accomplished or done in the past. These thoughts will not allow us to move forward and enjoy life as it comes. However, we CAN use those thoughts as fuel to help us get where we want to be. We can enjoy our mornings and be grateful for each waking moment. We can have time in the mornings to praise the Lord for the blessings He has given to us. We do not have to wake up in a reactive state. It's a choice we all have. What will you choose?

Think about this:

> "A man who dares to waste one hour of life has not discovered the value of life."
>
> - Charles Darwin

To this day, waking up early makes me feel good. Why? Because it gives me more time in the day. While school is in session, I *HAVE* to wake my daughter up at a certain time (at least until she is old enough to wake up on her own). I *COULD* wait until right before I have to wake her up to get myself up, but then I would start my day stressed and overwhelmed. I used to do that all the time and it was a horrible way to start the day. In knowing that, I now *CHOOSE* not to start my day in a negative state. I want to have the chance to be positive, to think positively, and to start my day happy. I have learned techniques that allow me to be in a better state before I have to actually start my day. This has been a pivotal and very important point in my life.

Now, if you don't have kids or a family, then maybe you can get away with waking up later and ending your day on a positive note. That is fine. If that works for you, then go for it. Just don't tell me you *CAN'T* wake up earlier or that you *DON'T* have time. We make time for things that are important to us. You have time. It's just not a priority. Let's be honest.

2.2. Establish a Good Routine

> *"Brothers and sisters, I do not consider myself yet to have taken hold of it. But one thing I do; Forgetting what is behind and straining toward what is ahead."*
>
> - Philippians 3:13

So how does it begin?

Consider this: studies show it is better to start your day off in a more positive state because it dictates the rest of your day. I challenge you to think about what might REALLY be better for you ... maybe if you change your schedule up, you will find that you are a more positive person to be around. Ask people who are around you all the time. See what they say. Maybe, just maybe, you will want to change things up a bit. We don't often notice our own faults. Accept some constructive feedback from others. I am happier all day because of the way I start my day ... I know that.

Let's explore one of our team member's success stories. Carolyn was exhausted, but decided she wanted to finally get on track. We had a great consultation, where we talked about her life and her goals. We talked about how you have to take things one step at a time. We talked about changing your mindset and working on time management. Carolyn realized that she often felt overwhelmed. As the mom of a 2-yr-old and 7-month-old, she was just exhausted all the time. Mom, wife, student ... and then try to engage in a new lifestyle? How was all this going to work?

Carolyn reached out after following my journey for a while and allowed me to give her tools to help with her own endeavors. We talked about her stress and feelings of being overwhelmed quite often. She admitted that when she has a ton to do, she often shuts down. She is in good company, because I am EXACTLY the same way if I'm not careful! I had to become aware of my own actions so I could begin to change them. The first step is awareness. Once we become aware of our actions, we can begin to take steps to change the outcome and how we handle situations.

I can't even count the amount of times I have just completely felt so overwhelmed that I just didn't do anything. Did that make me feel better or worse? Of course, worse ... and even more overwhelmed. Did the issues go away? NO! Did the tasks take care of themselves? NO! So how was I helping the situation by shutting down? I didn't! I made it worse! On top of that, I found myself not exercising AND not eating like I should have been. I simply wasn't putting in the effort. I can honestly say this went in cycles. I had highs that were super high and lows that felt like I wasn't going to get out of them. But, I did. How did I do that?

Time management and schedules. I began to realize how valuable time is so I didn't waste it quite as much. I also began to take account of what I was doing so that I could take more control of it all.

An old Chinese Proverb states, "One cannot manage too many affairs: like pumpkins in the water, one pops up while you try to hold down the other."

Is this something that will just magically make everything ok? Nope. You have to put forth the effort to realize you are NOT a super hero and you are NOT expected to be one. You are human! God gave us the gift to get a lot done at one time, but He also gave us the Sabbath. We all need to rest some and we are NOT expected to take on every situation with flying colors 24/7. You will only get a few tasks done in a day because, as we all know, life happens. So, control what you can control and give the rest to God. Schedule your day, but allow some time for "life" to happen. We can only control ourselves through faith, patience, and self-awareness. That's it. We can't control anyone or anything else and we shouldn't expend extra energy trying to. Until we realize this and put it to memory ... and utilize it daily ... we will NOT achieve total health and happiness in our lives. We will constantly be chasing harmony instead of being still every now and then and allowing fulfillment to come into our lives. We must learn to be grateful and understanding that we are not perfect and we are not superhuman. We do what we can, we give it to God, and we press forward knowing that He is guiding us the entire way through.

Most of how we operate is due to our subconscious mind. There is some research that suggests our subconscious minds were developed by the age of seven. Everything after that went to our conscious mind. When our subconscious mind operates, we are in what we often refer to as "automatic." Our conscious mind is what tells us we can't do something or that we will fail if we try. That is fear. We can turn this off or we can allow it to destroy us. The choice is ours.

> *"For the Spirit God gave us does not make us timid, but gives us power, love, and self-discipline."*
> — 2 Timothy 1:7

While it takes time to develop new information into our subconscious mind, it isn't impossible. Much of what we do on a daily basis goes back to what we have learned over time. We can use this tool for just about anything.

Is that television show that you're watching going to get you closer to your goals? Is shutting down going to get that paper you have due written? Are your kids going to need you no matter how overwhelmed you already feel? These are the questions you have to ask yourself.

Consider the following verse when you begin to feel overwhelmed. Become aware of the signs you are beginning to shut down. Once you have become aware, you can take the necessary steps to calm down and not allow yourself to give up:

> *"When you pass through the waters, I will be with you; and when you pass through the rivers, they will not sweep over you. When you walk through the fire, you will not be burned; the flames will not set you ablaze."*
> — Isaiah 43:2

Most of my life, I did not realize that He was not going to give me more than I could handle. While I would tend to give up at times, He allowed me to keep going. He will do the same for you if you allow Him in your heart.

One thing I had to learn was that I was NOT expected to keep my house squeaky clean as a mom and an entrepreneur. If you walk into my house now, you will see that I don't have it all tidy. Would I like to? Of course. But it's not a priority. I have learned to prioritize. I am a mom first. I am a wife, and I am also an entrepreneur. I also need to somehow keep myself healthy so I can be around longer for my kid and because I want people to know that I am walking the walk right alongside them. If I let myself go, who is going to want to listen to anything I have to say? I have to practice what I preach. Now, at age 41, I am finally doing just that.

Even when I "looked" healthy on the outside, I was not happy on the inside. There were so many things I needed to work on mentally, but I didn't know where to start. I finally sought out those who have been on the same journey. I listened and began to take necessary steps to change my outcome. I read books, listened to podcasts, and took steps towards becoming more open to possibilities. The number one thing I did was give my life to God. I partnered with Him because I got to the point where I no longer lean on my own understanding. Proverbs 3:5-6 says, *"Trust in the Lord with all your heart and lean not on your understanding. In all your ways, acknowledge Him, and He shall direct your paths."* I took this verse to heart. I began to work on myself from the inside out. That is what got me to where I am now. It didn't matter that I was going to the gym and eating healthy ... I was mentally self-sabotaging. It wasn't healthy at all. I would waste time on social media trying to see what others were doing so I could do the same. I began to conform. I wanted to be "liked" and appreciated. This was NOT what I needed to be wasting time on.

I had to change myself. I had to change my thoughts and how I perceived things. If I had a lot to get done, I started waking up earlier. I formed a schedule and stuck to it. I allowed time for "life" and only sought out to reach about 3-4 other tasks each day, so that I did not feel like it was unfathomable. I place a star by the top 3 tasks I need to get accomplished that day and that allows me to feel accomplished at the end of the day instead of completely overwhelmed.

Time management and mindset go hand and hand. You can't manage your time if you aren't working on your mindset. You won't achieve the tasks you set out to do if you don't believe in yourself. It starts here. Awareness is taking action steps to change the outcome of your situation so that you achieve more in a day than you did before.

I always hear people tell me they don't have time, but I don't hear people say, "I don't have time, but I'd like to learn how to find more time." Maybe if they started the conversation on a more positive note, they wouldn't shut down my ideas before we even start. If welcomed, I encourage everyone I have a conversation with to be successful.

We simply must learn how to balance life with goals. This goes for anything you do. In the case of exercise, if you work full time and have kids, involve your kids in your workouts. Show them what an active lifestyle looks like. Be the example. When I first began my journey after having our daughter, I was working full time and going to school full time. She was a baby. I would use her as my weight and do what I could. Later on, she became more active and we did things together. We learned how to motivate each other and she learned how to be an active and healthy kid. She made a great weight and she had so much fun with me lifting her up in the air and climbing on my back while I attempted planks and push-ups. After a few years went by, I realized I was indeed teaching her how to live an active lifestyle. I wasn't having to reach my goals without her. I was reaching them with her.

When I did my first bodybuilding show while working full time and being a single mom while my husband was moving to another country, I included her in my meal preps and active lifestyle. We would go to the track on the weekends and climb stairs together. When we got to Japan, it continued. I was molding her into this amazingly active kid just by including her. Now, when I watch her, I think about all that and how it made this lifestyle normal for her. I now do the same in my business. I include her more. I have had people ask me how I keep my business and family life separate. I don't. I include my family more and I actually involve them in decisions and operations. My daughter helps me with ideas and my husband helps with his design and critical thinking abilities. I enjoy receiving assistance from those who have abilities I do not possess.

So, when you start feeling overwhelmed about finding time, look for ways you can intertwine certain things in your life to help accomplish more than one thing at a time. Be a parent, but be active. It's definitely possible. Think about what you are going to write that paper about while you're going for a walk. Talk to your family about things. You don't have to be alone. Have a support system. If you involve them more, they will most likely feel more comfortable in involving you as well. It's a two-way street. Treat people like you want to be treated. Open up to those who you care about and who care about you. Let them in.

Do a time audit. Where do you spend most of your time (See worksheet for more assistance in this area)?

Think of three things that distract you from your most important tasks. Become "aware" of those things so you can notice when you are becoming distracted.

Make more time if you need to. Make time to take care of yourself.

Waking up earlier. It's not for everyone, but it has definitely been a game changer for me!

Here is a win from my client, Carolyn. This was her first win and the first of many to come:

> "Jodi, thank you so much for your advice about blocking out time for tasks and prioritizing. Tonight was a night I knew would be rough. I had to cook, clean, get both kids to bed, and finish a project and assignment for two classes between 6-9pm. I was so overwhelmed. Normally, I'd try to avoid the tasks until 8pm or later, and by then it has become unrealistic and just adds to my stress – but tonight, I tried blocking out time for each task and I GOT IT DONE! It is 8:30pm and I am done for the night, and accomplished more than I often do in a day. Thank you for that piece of advice, I am really proud of myself tonight."

I am proud of her too! This was the first step to her new success.

All she had to do was implement a few things that I had to learn also. I am able to relate to most people because pretty much everything they have or are going through is something I experienced as well. They say experience is the best teacher. It surely is! Through what God has taken me through and pulled me out of, I am now able to share with the world some of the things that took me YEARS to learn. Don't be as stubborn as I was. It won't happen overnight, but every little step you take towards ultimate achievement will be what will get you where you want to be each day.

It starts with awareness, but you must have a positive attitude. Make a schedule the night before and write down just a few tasks that will allow you to achieve what you have to get done. Prioritization is key! Managing your time is key! Not allowing things that are out of your control is so important! Doing this on a consistent basis will be the game changer for anyone.

Look at all the areas in your life you spend time on. Evaluate areas you may need to leave alone for a bit. Maybe it's social media. Maybe it's that television show you always watch. If you have to put these things down in order to have more time for yourself and your family and/or friends, so be it. Look at the people you surround yourself with. Are you allowing them to steal your time? If so, maybe there are some boundaries that need to be set.

This was an issue for me, especially since I am a natural "people pleaser." Nevertheless, I had to realize the more time I GAVE away to those who weren't as important as some of the other things in my life, the less time I had to get things done that had to be done at the end of the day. Make your schedule and stick to it. Now, I do have a couple friends that I will allow myself to change the course of my day. These are people who would do the same for me. I know they would. However, I also have to ensure I get the most important tasks completed before I do that as well. This is another reason for waking up earlier. Get as much done as possible as early as possible. That way, when things come up that may change your original schedule, you still have some flexibility to be successful for that day.

Mainly, be open to becoming aware of the things that are taking your time away. Once you do this, you have begun to control the one area of your life most people don't have a handle on. If you look at the high-performing people in the world, they do have control over this area. If you want to be a high-performer, you have to be willing to put forth effort in this area and help your outcome. You CAN do it. You just have to make it important enough to WANT to do it. God believes in you. He wants us all to be successful. He does not want us to live stressful, overwhelming lives. I believe in you. Do you?

Chapter 3
Self-Care and Positivity

3.1 Stop Worrying About the Day as Soon as You Wake Up

Open Your Eyes in the Morning and Say "Thank You" for Everything You Have.

> *"Devote yourselves to prayer, being watchful and thankful."*
> – Colossians 4:2

We began this conversation in Chapter 2, but we really need to continue it more in depth.

When you wake up in the morning, how many of you are panicked and stressed first thing? I have people tell me all the time how they hit snooze or oversleep. I used to do that too! Where did it get me though? I can honestly say that not sleeping in and giving myself time to do things more now is so much better for my sanity. When you wake up in a panic, it sets the stage for the rest of your day. Before I found the routine I now have, instead of being able to take a moment to be thankful for what I had and thinking about what made me happy, what I am proud of myself for getting accomplished, what I am enjoying and committed to in my life, I would wake up and immediately start listing out all the things I needed to get done that day. I was stressing myself out before the day even started. If you wake up late, you are even more stressed because you weren't able to list out your tasks. Now what?! You've completely set yourself up for failure that day. I know. I am telling you this is exactly what I used to do. What I should have been doing and what I hope you will start doing is listing out everything the night before. That way, it's already there and we can rest assured knowing we have already done our planning for the next day. We have already looked at our schedule. We already know what is coming up. We can prioritize (because no matter how much we think we can get done in the course of the day, things come up and often times, we aren't going to get it all done).

So how do we get around the anxiety?

There are ways to focus on how you wake up in the morning. If you have already worked on your mindset and time management, you already overcame the initial feelings of being overwhelmed and stressed. You are waking up a little earlier, and now you have time to focus on the good in your life instead of all the things you have to do as soon as you wake up. You are more relaxed and you are crushing your morning. Now consider these tips to help you even more:

- Consider what makes you happy
- Give gratitude
- Relax your body
- Focus on breathing
- Don't attach to your negative thoughts
- Stay off social media
- Prepare a delicious breakfast
- Establish a meditation practice
- Don't check your phone until much later
- Do something physical (go for a run or do some sort of cardio, yoga, or something that will allow you to feel more energized first thing)
- Create a routine that includes morning self-care
- Wake up to a clean room (tidy up the night before so you don't wake up with chores to do)
- Ask yourself, "How can I make today amazing?"
- Smile regardless of how you might feel at first[5]

Challenge yourself to stay off your phone the first hour of the day. I am still working on this. I tend to use my phone for my devotion – but then

I go to my social media. Having my phone around me allows me to stray. Therefore, I need to find another way to fulfill my devotion. This is something I will work on. What I have stopped doing is checking messages, Facebook, or emails the first hour. I wait until I am in a positive state of mind. That way, if anyone sends me something negative, I don't react. I just close it and move forward.

What would you rather be? Proactive or Reactive? The choice is yours.

How do you know which one you are? Examine your morning routine. Do you have one? We all do. Does yours serve you in a positive or negative manner?

How can you change? The first step is becoming more aware.

Time to dig in ... the decision is yours ... you are in control of one person at all times: YOU

According to the website, Vocabulary.com, "If you are **proactive**, you make things happen, instead of waiting for them to happen to you. Active **means** "doing something." The prefix pro- **means** "before." If you are **proactive**, you are ready before something happens. The opposite is being **reactive**, or waiting for things to unfold before responding."[14]

Which one do you think is going to help you more in life?

Being proactive is doing things like building a schedule for yourself to ensure you finish your tasks for the day AND create the time to work on yourself – whether that be exercise and nutrition, school, reading a personal development book – whatever it may be. You are the person who gets stuff done because you are not making excuses for why you don't have time to do extra things in your life. Think about that as you continue to read.

Maya Angelou once said, "If you don't like something, change it. If you can't change it, change your attitude." The number of things you accomplish or don't accomplish in your life is directly related to your attitude. Life is life. There is absolutely NOTHING you can do about some of the things that happen to you in life. However, instead of thinking about how it is happening TO you, why not think about it as life happening FOR you? Think about everything that has happened in your life. Everything you have gone through has made you the person you are today. Are you proud of that person or not? If not, CHANGE IT! Make it to where you can be proud! Stop living in fear. Stop living your life to be comfortable and get out of your comfort zone. There is something in you that is telling you that there is more in life for you than you are allowing at this time.

Take ownership in your life. Ask God to help you create the life you want. If you are an unhappy person and good things are happening, you will create more unhappiness. Think about it. This happens more than we realize. This has happened to me so many times I can't even count. The more things would happen, the more I shut down. By the time I was in my mid-30's, I had so much I should have been grateful for. Instead, I was still searching for meaning in my life. It took me up until about the age of 38 before I finally started realizing the only person who was making the negative in my life thrive was me. By this time, people who did not know me, thought I had it together. I was far from having it all together. I was still lost and chasing what I THOUGHT I was supposed to do and who I THOUGHT I was supposed to be.

One day I finally woke up and said enough was enough. When we see people on social media, they may "look" happy. They "look" healthy. The thing we don't realize is that total health doesn't just include what you look like on the outside. It's how you feel. It's the light that allows you to glow on a regular basis. It's the natural happiness that occurs when you are finally letting go of the fear that is holding you back and you decide to take action in your life to make it better.

The journey is continuous. There is NEVER a linear path. You will constantly have to make choices. A famous quote from Law of Attraction Coaching states, "doubt kills more dreams than failure ever will." We are going to fail. It is inevitable. It has taken me years to finally allow myself to be successful, but I have to get out there and stop being afraid to fail. I am going to fail. The failures are what make me better. The failures are what drive me to become better. If we just go out and crush it every day, there is no challenge. We have nothing else to work for. That is not an exciting life. Failure is the driver that allows us to crush our dreams and believe in ourselves more each day.

"And without doubt the lesser is blessed by the greater."
- Hebrews 7:7

Maybe you are at a point in your life where you have a fear of the unknown. I was there on so many occasions. I have held myself back from so many things and even to this day, I continue to struggle with confidence in certain areas. Nevertheless, I know that I have to continue. I have to fail my way to success. I have to keep my head up, be proud of the person I am today, be proud of all the adversity and the mistakes God has allowed me to make. I have to take ownership of my own actions. I have to know that through Him, I have the capability to control one person-me. I have the ability to be in control of how I react to things I encounter in life.

So, are you going to be proactive or reactive? Are you going to wait for life to happen to you so that you can get flustered and frustrated when things don't go your way? Or are you going to take control, schedule your day, take time for you, and learn how to be appreciative of the things you have instead of focusing on what you don't have?

Think about the way you are living your life now. Do you operate from a proactive state or are you a reactive being? Think about a recent incident that left you in a reactive state. Write about it here:

Fact is, humans are naturally reactive. It takes more effort to become proactive. It also takes work to stay in a positive state. Therefore, if you are a reactive person, you are also a lazy person. I was lazy. I thought everything should just come to me. *"In the same way, faith by itself, if it is not accompanied by action, is dead."* (James 2:17). I had already put so much effort into everything I did. Why was it not just happening? Why did I have to continue doing even more work? Fact is, it wasn't until I started being proactive that things started happening for the better. I began walking in faith. The vision is there and He has a plan. All I have to do is go when He tells me to go and sit still when He tells me to sit still.

I have made the choice to be proactive for as long as I live, because having lived most of my life in the reactive state was miserable. It was depressing. I never got where I wanted to be. I was in a job I didn't necessarily like. I had no control over my schedule. All I could do was hold on and keep going. I was in control of my own destiny, but I kept saying I wasn't.

I have now focused on developing my mind. I surround myself with quality people. I don't stay in a negative state. I look at what I have in life instead of what I don't have. I am living a total health life because I have chosen to be the type of person who is no longer driven by fear. Living in fear has kept me from my true destiny for far too long.

Are you going to make a choice today to put in the effort to allow yourself to be happy? I give you permission to be happy. It's ok. If you have family or people around you who you love, you must allow yourself to be happy. Why? Because how is anyone around you going to be happy if you aren't? Whether you know it or not, living in a reactive state also tends to make you give off negative energy. If you are continuously giving negative energy, do you think you are positively influencing your family and friends? There's no way!

It's time you put yourself to the test. Stop being afraid to fail. Stop limiting yourself. Plan and schedule so you no longer say "I don't have the time." We all have 24 hours in a day. How are you going to use YOUR time? Today is the day. Someday doesn't exist. It's time to get yourself in a place to where you can truly fulfill your destiny. I am right here beside you doing the same. Together, we will get through life and we will take it as it comes ... and we WILL win!

Here are a couple more steps that I have started implementing:

- Rest as deeply as possible so when the alarm goes off, you are ready to go (don't go to bed stressed about how you will take on your tasks for the next day, shut down your phone/laptop at least 30 minutes before you plan to lie down, read a relaxing book or listen to some relaxing music to help you get into sleep mode, turn off the lights and silence any distractions ... also, stop drinking lots of water or liquids at least 30 minutes before time to lie down so you aren't up in the middle of the night having to use the restroom)
- Have a bottle of water by the bed in case you wake up thirsty (just sip if it's the middle of the night), but especially so you can drink it first thing in the morning; hydration first thing in the morning is an amazing feeling!
- Splash some cold water on your face and especially around your eyes; get the sleeps out of your eyes and begin to feel awake
- Be ready to conquer the day by giving thanks for all you have
- Remember this:
    o God First
    o Me Second
    o Everyone Else Third (Family)
    o Career (School, Work, Other Obligations) Fourth

If you can operate in that order, you will be good to go. It takes time, but it is so worth it to be able to take better control of your mornings so that you can operate better during the day and manage stress and life as it comes to you. Become aware of how you operate so that you can begin to take steps to control your actions. Believe me, it will make a WORLD of difference!

These are some tips that will help you crush your morning. You will begin to notice how much a morning of positivity impacts your day over a morning of stress and anxiety. Which one would you rather have?

For me, it was a no brainer. I have worked on these things each day. I have reminder lists in my room, in my kitchen, and in my office. These lists help me implement new things into my routine and remind me of how I need to spend my mornings. Just in case I start to fall off, I can go back to the list and remind myself what I need to be doing in order to have a better start to my day.

Those are ways to implement positivity into your life. So how do you allow yourself to take care of you when you have others who are relying on you to take care of them?

Have you ever been a caretaker for someone? Or are you a parent? If you're a parent, you always have one or more people to take care of. Do you give yourself the opportunity to take care of you first or do you allow the others to get all of you to where, by the time you do want to do something for yourself, you forget? Why do you forget? You forget because it isn't normal for you to take care of you. We are so programmed to just take care of everyone else.

We want to be accepted and loved. We yearn for outside appreciation. So, we bend over backwards for everyone else in order to get approval. The problem is, when we neglect our own personal needs, we end up eventually feeling like we are unworthy. We begin to tell ourselves that what we want doesn't matter. We continue to work hard for everyone else's approval and continue to neglect ourselves. We suppress feelings so as not to hurt others. We worry so much about others that we can literally make ourselves sick. If this is a possibility, why don't we put that much effort into ourselves?

Most of us aren't even aware that we put ourselves on the backburner unless we begin to analyze our health habits. We say things like, "I don't have time to exercise or meal prep." In reality, we aren't willing to take some extra time and help ourselves out. I used to be the same way! I would help everyone else and be there for everyone else, but then it was ME that was getting the short end of the stick. If we are not willing to take care of ourselves, how do we expect to live each day to the fullest? How can we show up for everyone else? Maybe it makes us happy to take care of others, but are we truly fulfilled?

Think about how you spend your time. Do a time audit. Does your time audit include self-care? If not, I strongly urge you to begin including it into your daily regimen. Otherwise, you are going to end up sick and tired and not knowing why. It's because you aren't taking care of yourself.

Yes, we have obligations we must fulfill to others. However, if we are not fulfilling our own needs, is that really going to allow us to do what we need to do? When we aren't taking care of ourselves, we are setting ourselves up for resentment and negative thoughts. We are tired because we aren't eating the foods that will give us energy because we weren't willing to take the time to prepare them and keep them will us.

My challenge to you is to read over the next portion of this chapter and begin taking care of yourself. Do the extra things that are required to feel good about yourself all-around. Start out by writing down one thing you will do for yourself each day. It doesn't have to be huge. It just has to be something. Are you going to eat breakfast? Are you going to say positive things to yourself? Are you going to go to the spa for a little bit or exercise? What is that one thing you are going to do today? Begin here and see how being consistent in this area can ultimately change your life.

Here are some steps to take if you know you need to begin implementing self-care into your life:

1. Believe you are worthy – REALLY believe it. Don't just say it. You have to BELIEVE it!

2. Wake up a little earlier (10 to 15 minutes) and be grateful for your life. Get clear on your goals and allow your follow-up actions to be towards those goals.

3. Stay off your phone at least for the first 30 minutes of the day (as mentioned above). Did you know that your brain is in its prime during the first 20 minutes of being awake? What are you feeding your brain in that first 20 minutes? Positivity and motivation or checking on everyone else?

As you may have noticed, a lot of this stems from the chapter on Time Management. Taking control of your time allows you to also take care of yourself. Think about the things in your life that make you happiest. Allow those thoughts to be the first thing on your mind when you wake up. Learn to think more about what you have rather than what you lack. Just in doing this, you may find that it becomes easier for you to have a better attitude and want to take care of yourself. Think about those people in your life who would be affected if you were no longer here. Allow those thoughts to be your motivation – your drivers for success and health.

> *"He helps tired people be strong. He gives power to those without it."*
>
> – Isaiah 40:29

Always remember, no matter what, you are enough. He made you to be something more than you could ever imagine. When times get rough and you can't find the path to keep going, rely on His guidance. He will carry you through.

3.2 Say "Thank You" for Everything You Have

> *"Whatever happens, always be thankful. This is how God wants you to live in Christ Jesus."*
>
> – 1 Thesselonians 5:18

Today is your day. Your negativity must end here.

Towards the beginning of last year, I was miserable. I wasn't able to pay my bills, I was trying to rebuild my business in a city where the market was saturated, I was learning how to be a solo mom (my husband and I were separated due to his obligation to the U.S. Air Force and eligibility to retire). I was told I would not be able to retire from the Air Force. My life was changed completely. It was not the first time I was in this place – but it was the last.

See, before I finally ditched my bad attitude, I was only looking at what I didn't have. Comparing myself to what I used to have and who I used to be. I would compare myself to others. Why didn't I have what they had? I worked hard. I lived a life filled with turmoil. I was here on a mission to change lives. So why was it so difficult for me to have what "they" had.

The problem was, due to the comparisons to others, I was only making things worse for myself.

I was listening to a podcast about this very subject by Ed Mylett and it really got me thinking. It's so true: our unhappiness stems from the comparisons we make on a daily basis.

The problem is, we are allowing the comparisons to pull us down even further. We are allowing them to dictate how to proceed. We are allowing them to take over our mental stability. We shut down because of them. We decide, "today, I am just going to sit here and watch tv, because that will make me feel better."

In reality, the underlying issue is still there. We haven't solved anything by trying to hide from it. We do what another renowned speaker said recently – we "non-confront." We say things like, "if I just drink this beer and hang out, all my problems will go away – I will FEEL better." But do you really? Do the problems really go away, or are they just temporarily put on hold?

Think about it for a minute – how often are your thoughts in a negative state? Use this space to think and journal about this:

I am truly grateful that I have been led by a higher being so I no longer have to rely on my own inner thoughts. I could not have picked myself up. Someone picked me up. I did have to look into the mirror, though. Who was I trying to fool? I wasn't fooling anyone? I didn't smile much. I was just unhappy. But it was ME who was making me unhappy.

Once I began to take the steps into trusting the Lord and allowing Him to guide me, everything changed. I began to pray about EVERYTHING. Better people started coming into my life. They gave me hope. I realized that I was the person my daughter was looking up to. How could I let her down by being in a negative state all the time? How can I tell her to be grateful for what she has if I am not doing the same? How could I do that to her? How often do we not practice what we preach? Take some time to ponder this. I know I was guilty. The Lord provides me with all these concepts that allow me to be a better person. He has provided me with these gifts and this knowledge that allows me to help others change their lives. So why on earth was I not using ALL the information I have learned throughout my life? I began using scriptures to help guide me. This is something I had NOT tried yet. I began to realize those who were happy and fulfilled believed in the Lord and the power He has.

> *"Using the scriptures, those who serve God will be prepared and will have everything they need to do every good work."*
>
> - 2 Timothy 3:17

In relying on my own understanding, the problems weren't going away. They would compound. I thought if I just put them to the side, they would go away. That was definitely NOT the case. They just got worse because I kept thinking about what I *used* to have and where I *used* to be - comparisons. This is no way to operate. Our lives are built upon seasons. There will be some great seasons and there will be some trying seasons. This is all a test for you to strengthen you and allow you to get where the Lord needs you to be. This is what had to happen for me to realize I have so much to be grateful for.

Before I knew the Lord, I would stress about things that hadn't even happened yet. I had to get out of that state of mind before the whole world came crashing down. During all this, people who didn't know me thought I was fine. I put on a front. I faked it. I smiled when I wanted to cry.

Again, this was not the first time I was confronted by my own self-sabotage. Therefore, I knew when it got bad, I had to pick myself up. I had to walk in Faith. I had to let go of the comparisons of who I wanted to be and focus on who I am. I have more than so many people. I have a roof over my head and even when times are tough financially, I figure something out. I find a way to make things happen. I know that walking around the problem isn't going to fix the problem.

So today, I challenge you to stop comparing yourself, your relationships, your business, your job, and your financial situation to others. Stop comparing it to what you *used* to have. Start putting one foot in front of the other and focus more on what you COULD have if you actually started confronting life instead of trying to walk around it. You can never just be a passerby in this thing we call life. You and I are IN IT. We are what makes this world continue.

Choose today whether you are going to be that person on the street who does what everyone else does and smiles a fake smile, or are you going to think about what you have, the fact you are alive and well, and smile that smile that gives you and the others around your life? I will tell you, smiling the real smile has made me a happier person all around. I have also noticed that it makes others around me happier. When you see someone walking by and they look like they might not be having the greatest day, smile, say, "Hi, how are you?" and see how your positivity becomes contagious.

I have personally noticed that when I intentionally speak to someone out of the blue, it changes their attitude. Let's change the way we look at life, the way we compare ourselves and let the wrong visions pull us down. Instead, let the comparisons fuel your fire. That's what I had to do. I had to finally take a stand in my life, say enough is enough, and let the life I want be what gets me going day in and day out.

Is it perfect? Is everyday peachy? Not at all. Nevertheless, by implementing the things I talk about all the time – starting the day thinking about what you have instead of what you don't have, smiling even when you may not want to smile, speaking to others around you and lifting *them* up, taking yourself out of the equation, and just being an all-around good person – you may find that you become more fulfilled in your life.

Do you know how many people are out there who have absolutely nothing, but are completely fulfilled? There are many. They don't need to have a whole lot. They just appreciate life. They embrace each day and deal with the battles as they come. They don't ask, "why is this happening to me?" They ask, "why is this happening FOR me?" Try it. It doesn't cost anything. Happiness is free. The Lord doesn't charge for mentorship. He *wants* to hear from us. He *waits* for us to call on Him. He will guide us through all of the "stuff" if we allow Him to. We just have to choose happiness over discontent and empty comparisons. *We* have to do that. No one else can do it for you.

Today is your day. Don't let it pass you by.

Remember this as you continue your reading and operate each day:

> *"Whoever dwells in the shelter of the Most High will rest in the shadow of the Almighty. I will say of the Lord, 'He is my refuge and my fortress, my God in whom I trust ... He will cover you will his feathers, and under his wings you will find refuge; his faithfulness will be your shield and rampart; You will not fear the terror of night, nor the arrow that flies by day, nor the pestilence that stalks in the darkness, nor the plague that destroys at midday ... If you say, 'The Lord is my refuge,' and you make the Most High your dwelling ..."*
> – Psalms 91:1-2, 4-6, 9-10

Be grateful, my friends. Today, tomorrow, and forever. This will allow you to see what the Lord has in store for you, just as He has shown me. When you come to Him, come to Him with thanksgiving and be humble. For He is the God Most High. He can only guide you if you humble yourself before Him. This is what I have learned and I felt obligated to share this with you as well.

Now let's talk about something that baffles everyone I talk to when it comes to health and wellness ... Nutrition.

Chapter 4
Basic Nutrition

4.1 Food Intake

> *"But the Lord told him, 'You may eat fruit from any tree in the garden, except the one that has the power to let you know the difference from right and wrong. If you eat any fruit from that tree, you will die before the day is over.'"*
>
> – Genesis 2:16-17

Think about the choices in food we have these days. Man built all these fast ways to eat. However, man did *not* think about how these options were going to negatively impact the world ... or maybe it was part of the master plan. The problem is, we are a people who will overindulge and not think about what we are doing to ourselves in the long run. Eating fast food isn't a bad thing. It's all about decisions and choices. For instance, I can go to a fast food restaurant and order foods that won't negatively impact my overall well-being. I also don't eat out all the time. It's all about moderation and making more sound choices. We tend to only think about what the food tastes like. So, what do the owners of these places do? They pump the foods with harmful ingredients that, if eaten in abundance, can have a negative impact on our overall health.

When God told Adam not to eat from the tree that allowed him to have choices, it wasn't because God didn't want Adam to have choices. God knew Adam, being a man, wouldn't make the right choices. God knew Adam would stray from what was right through the Lord. Think about all the people in the world now. God knew this would happen.

Man took and ran with all these ideas and now we are a people who are suffering with lethargy, metabolic disorders, coronary problems, cancers, etc. While some of these issues are genetic, we can definitely make it worse by taking in foods that will contribute to them. Food should be our friend, but many of us make it our enemy. In reality, all it takes is for us to make choices that will lead to a better, longer life. We need to make choices that will allow us to nourish our bodies internally and give us life.

Do you know what one of the easiest things you can do to become healthier is drink water? This is easy, right? Unfortunately, it's not easy for everyone. We didn't all grow up drinking water, and those of us who did probably didn't know just how important it was. As time went by, we strayed away from any good habits we may have developed as kids. We ended up doing things the "world" told us to do to help "stay awake" and we went after taste instead of providing the one ingredient our bodies need – water.

> One of the promises God makes in Psalms 73, is that He *"will bring his people back, and they will drink the water he so freely gives."*
>
> – Psalms 73:10

Think about the times we don't have free access to water – the natural disasters we are confronted with as God's way to attempt to wake us up. People who don't normally drink water are buying it up because they know it won't be available for long. We take the normal availability of water for granted, don't we?

It's time we utilize this resource to our full advantage when God provides it. Water is life.

In an article found on the USGS website, I found the following to help me convey the importance of this compound to our bodies:

Water is of major importance to all living things; in some organisms, up to 90% of their body weight comes from water. Up to 60% of the human adult body is water.

According to H.H. Mitchell, Journal of Biological Chemistry 158, the brain and heart are composed of 73% water, and the lungs are about 83% water. The skin contains 64% water, muscles and kidneys are 79%, and even the bones are watery: 31%.

Each day humans must consume a certain amount of water to survive. Of course, this varies according to age and gender, and also by where someone lives. Generally, an adult male needs about 3 liters (3.2 quarts) per day while an adult female needs about 2.2 liters (2.3 quarts) per day. All of the water a person needs does not have to come from drinking liquids, as some of this water is contained in the food we eat.

Water serves a number of essential functions to keep us all going

- A vital nutrient to the life of every cell, acts first as a building material.
- It regulates our internal body temperature by sweating and respiration
- The carbohydrates and proteins that our bodies use as food are metabolized and transported by water in the bloodstream;
- It assists in flushing waste mainly through urination
- acts as a shock absorber for brain, spinal cord, and fetus
- forms saliva
- lubricates joints

According to Dr. Jeffrey Utz, Neuroscience, pediatrics, Allegheny University, different people have different percentages of their bodies made up of water. Babies have the most, being born at about 78%. By one year of age, that amount drops to about 65%. In adult men, about 60% of their bodies are water. However, fat tissue does not have as much water as lean tissue. In adult women, fat makes up more of the body than men, so they have about 55% of their bodies made of water. Thus:

- Babies and kids have more water (as a percentage) than adults.
- Women have less water than men (as a percentage).
- People with more fatty tissue have less water than people with less fatty tissue (as a percentage).[13]

For those of you who know me, you know that I carry around a gallon water jug each day. This is my goal every day – to drink that gallon of water. Considering I used to be a kid who absolutely *hated* water, this is a pretty big deal. I went from being the kid whose mom had to literally *force* her to sit and drink a large cup of water to being the adult who only drinks water to the adult you never see without water. Just like everything else in life, it did *not* happen overnight.

When I played sports, we *always* drank water. It just became more "normal" as I got older. When I joined the military, they taught us more about the importance of drinking water. While that is *not* the only thing I drank back then, I did drink a lot more than ever before. The longer I worked outside in harsh environments, deployed to hot, humid places, and stayed active, the more water I drank. Over many years, it got to the point where I didn't really want to drink much else. I actually *enjoyed* drinking water. Looking back, I now realize how much of an impact water has on our bodies, as well as our skin. I used to have acne pretty badly and I still have oily skin. Since I drink a lot of water, my skin isn't dry. The benefits have become my motivation to remain consistent with drinking my water. Two elements that make up one of the most important compounds God gave us – it's up to us to use the elements to our benefit.

The longer I was alive, the more I learned about the importance of water. When I began bodybuilding, I learned how water impacted our vascular system and muscles. I learned how to use it, along with food, to reach my goals. It was truly amazing to see the results.

First of all, did you know that your muscles are 70% water? So, for those of you who say you want your muscles to "pop out," drink more water and see what begins to happen.

Here's an easy way to figure out how much water you need (if the above information is too confusing): according to studies, our bodies require approximately *half* our body weight (in pounds) in ounces of water *each day* to function properly. Therefore, if you weigh 200 pounds, you need to drink at least 100 ounces of water each day (for my overseas friends, that's about 3.8 – just make it 4 liters for easy counting – liters for every 45 kilograms approximately). If you find yourself getting prolonged headaches or becoming tired and lethargic, maybe it's because you aren't giving your brain what it needs to survive. Think about it. Let's proceed ...

Drinking water not only keeps your organs in better health, but it also maintains and speeds up cellular development, leading to an all-natural metabolism booster.

When people come to me for a weight loss program, the first thing I do is find out what they are currently doing. If they are not exercising at all and they are not drinking enough water, those are the first two things we conquer. They become the foundation for everything else. Before I worry about teaching someone how to lift weights or eat better, I have to get them at least moving first and drinking more water. The good thing about moving is the more you move, the thirstier you get. Your body requires you to hydrate. Therefore, when people start implementing more exercise into their lives, they also begin drinking more water.

Did you know that if you don't drink enough water for a long period of time, you could be doing harm to your kidneys, eventually causing them to shut down? Our liver and our kidneys filter everything in our bodies. Toxins that don't get filtered through our liver goes to our kidneys for filtration. Our bodies are NOT made of 70% of the following: coffee, soda, tea, juice, and everything else besides - you guessed it - WATER!

The next time you go out to eat, try to do something a little different ... order water to drink instead of whatever else you normally get. Not only will you save a few dollars, but you'll also save your kidneys. Think about it ... Benefits of drinking water: you save your kidneys, you have more energy (due to the natural metabolism boost), muscles are plumper, which in turn causes a loss in body fat (leaner muscles equal less body fat), clearer skin, healthier cells (helps with immunity and lessens the cellular deformities that cause various types of cancer), and provides the bloodstream with necessary fluid.

Bottom line, water is your friend. A gallon water jug is less than $1 at the store. Think about what you spend on coffee and soda or anything other than water. I'm sure the $1 won't kill you ... but not drinking more water could ...

Once we have implemented more water into our lives, it's time to learn how to moderate our foods. Let me be very clear here: it's not about deprivation or lack thereof. It's simply about becoming wiser in our choices.

Basic understanding begins with something most people don't even know about – Basal Metabolic Rate, or BMR. "The rate of energy expended at rest is measured as either the Basal Metabolic Rate, or BMR, or the Resting Metabolic Rate, referred to as RMR. The RMR differs slightly from the BMR. Researchers usually measure RMR three to four hours after a person eats or does significant physical work. RMR tends to be somewhat higher than BMR and is a more practical concept because the ideal conditions for measuring BMR are more difficult to meet."[10]

BMR is also the least amount of fuel you need each day to keep your body functioning properly. Therefore, when people begin extreme dieting, often they are neglecting the foundation to where it all begins – knowing your BMR. If you would like to know how to figure out how much fuel your body requires in a day, you can surely contact me, or simply go to the website, https://www.calculator.net/bmr-calculator.html, for a good calculator I use when I am educating my clients on this portion of things so they can remain consistent once their programs end (so they don't have to hire a coach forever).

Once you have figured out your BMR, it is important to realize you have to add a little more to the BMR in order to replenish the fuel you lose throughout the day. This is why we (professionals and calculators you find) use a multiplier called "activity level." This allows you to figure out how much energy you expend when you are active or depending on what you do for a living. For those of you who are very busy, have you ever forgotten to eat for hours on end? Do you start to feel tired? What's the first thing you do? Do you choose foods that will help replenish the energy you have lost, or do you simply choose whatever is quick and easy? Do you go to the snack machine that is filled with processed, sugary foods? How do you feel afterward? Maybe it helps you temporarily, but then what? Either you crash from all the sugar or it just isn't enough to *really* fuel you for the long haul. The reason I use the website above for this portion is because it has the ability to use the activity level multiplier right there on the page. It makes it super easy to figure out. That is where it all begins.

Think of calories as fuel. When you expend a ton of fuel, you need to replenish it. Filling your body with processed foods is not the answer. Our bodies can't process that food very well. Over time, we put our bodies in overdrive and it becomes difficult for our internal machines to operate as they are supposed to. Think of it as a vehicle that requires premium gasoline for optimal performance. If you continue to put the regular unleaded gasoline in, what will happen to that vehicle over time? It won't run as well as it is supposed to. You aren't putting the proper fuel type in it. It begins to wear down and eventually isn't going to be reliable. Our bodies can easily go into this same category if we continue to make choices that aren't beneficial to the overall performance of our internal makeup.

While there are plenty of websites out there providing information on what I have covered here, I do advise anyone who wants to get started in learning how to eat to consult a trained professional who specializes in nutrition so that you are sure to get the correct information and do not become overwhelmed. When I first started my journey, it was truly overwhelming. Nevertheless, the more I became *interested*, the more I wanted to know. Now, I am truly grateful God allowed me to gain the knowledge in this area to not only maintain my *own* health, but to help others as well. Notice how I put the word *interested* in there. Human sciences have become a very interesting subject to me. That is why I am constantly doing research and why I know what I know. The Lord gave me passion in this area so that I would not lose sight of the mission and I would continue to yearn for more. For someone who absolutely did *not* like science in school, becoming addicted to learning more about it is a blessing.

4.2 How to Eat

> *"You have given great advice and wonderful wisdom to someone truly in need."*
>
> – Job 26:3

Time to learn how to moderate our food intake. It's not about deprivation or lack. God doesn't want us to *lack* anything. It's simply about becoming wiser in our choices.

> *"I, wisdom, dwell together with prudence; I possess knowledge and discretion. To fear the Lord is to hate evil; I hate pride and arrogance, evil behavior and perverse speech. Counsel and sound judgement are mine; I have insight, I have power."*
>
> – Proverbs 8:12-14

Anytime others would second-guess me or think I was telling them to track their foods because I did *not* want to help them, I would allow it to bother me. I would have people ask me why I wouldn't just give them a meal plan to follow. I've had people tell me tracking their food intake was too hard. For a while, I allowed this to begin changing things. Maybe I should create them a meal plan. Maybe I should just make it easier for them. However, what the Lord has provided me with now is confidence and knowledge. Giving a meal plan may allow them to take the easy road, but it won't actually *teach* them anything.

One of the things I have always done with my clients is *educated* them. As I mentioned earlier, I am not one to conform, so why should I start doing that now? I had to realize that I am *not* the coach for everyone and those who come to me will be those who truly *want* to gain insight and wisdom they can not only use for the rest of their lives, but they can also *share with others*. I want to *empower* people to become their best selves. I don't want them to have to rely on a coach forever. At some point, they have to be able to rely on *themselves*. Hence, the food diary.

So, before you decide to skip over this part of the book, I challenge you to read with an open mind. I have already prayed over you. The

Lord has given you the strength to try new things. All you have to do is be *willing*.

4.3 Diary Tracking

> *"And let us consider how we may spur one another on toward love and good deeds, not giving up meeting together, as some are in the habit of doing, but encouraging one another – and all the more as you see the Day approaching."*
>
> – Hebrews 10:24-25

Through my own experience, I learned that keeping a food diary was the absolute best way to learn how to eat. The reason is because in seeing what you are eating, you know if you are meeting your body's needs. People who guess what they are eating normally don't have the best results because they have no way of knowing what they are putting into their body. For moms, we tend to eat on the fly, not really knowing what we are eating, but just eating as we are on the run ... or NOT eating at all. It is so important to fuel our bodies correctly.

This is where time management and scheduling come into play. How do you get people to do something they haven't done before? In 2009, a group of researchers funded by the National Institutes of Health published a study of a different approach to weight loss. They ... assembled a group of 1600 obese people and asked them to concentrate on writing down everything they ate at least ONE DAY per week.[4]

According to this research, the one difference in what they did sparked several other healthy habits. The subjects would walk more and eat healthier snacks. They did this because when they logged their food, they started noticing certain patterns and they wanted to change their behaviors. The key here is they WANTED to change. No one was making them do this. They wanted to do it on their own. Many of the subjects started keeping food journals everyday over time. After six months, those "who kept daily food journals lost twice as much weight as everyone else."[3]

When I talk to people about tracking their food, I always get a sigh or a crazy look. Seriously. It's one more thing to add to your already busy schedule, right? Why on earth would you ever want to do that? Well, if you aren't willing to put a little effort into this, don't be surprised when you are getting the same results you've always been getting.

So, what does it take to start tracking your foods?

There are many diary tracking apps out there these days. A great app to use (and what my clients use because it allows me to hold them accountable) is called My Fitness Pal. The app is not foolproof, but it is enough to get you started. If you are working towards specific goals, hiring a trained professional and allowing him/her to assist you with your numbers is a great way to begin the learning process. This person has gone through the training already and knows how to guide you properly so you are not having to play the guessing game, getting frustrated, and quitting. Regardless of whether you hire help or try to do it on your own, the app is a great tool to use when it comes to tracking food. It has a barcode scanner I absolutely love (even scanned the Japanese food when we were located in Okinawa, Japan) and it has a huge database of food so you aren't having to try to figure out what you are eating when you are out and about.

Isn't all this stressful?

My answer: only if you allow it to be by not planning ahead and not doing it. Just as anything else in life, the more you do it, the better you get. It was a pain for me to track my foods when I first started my journey. I'd get to the end of the day and realize I forgot to add in a meal. I did not have anyone giving me tips or guiding me as I went along. All I knew was that it was the only way I was going to learn and that it has been proven on so many levels to be the one thing that works to help people actually UNDERSTAND nutrition. No one said any of this was going to be easy. All I will say is that once you begin implementing the things that work into your life, you may be amazed at the results. There are ways to ensure you are able to get your food diary completed even with a super busy schedule. Here are some hacks you can use:

1) KNOW YOUR WHY

Why are you doing this? Why did you download the app and/or hire a coach to help you? What are your goals and why have you made this step to secure your health? Now that you have read those questions, write them down – NOW! Think about your answers and write them down also. Make them real. Don't just let them be an idea in your head. Once you have done this, have the questions and answers hanging up in your kitchen, in your bedroom, in your living room – wherever you need to have them where you will see them every morning when you wake up. Look at them each morning first thing. It is important that we understand our goals and why they exist. If we just "say" we want to do something, but never make it real, we make it easy to simply "forget" about them or say things like, "I didn't do it today, so I will start tomorrow." Tomorrow becomes the next day, and so on and so forth. Here's one fact for you – SOMEDAY is not a day of the week. If you got to this point where you knew tracking your foods would get you closer to your goals a bit faster, wouldn't you want to explore that? Is making excuses and not taking action going to get you there? Not at all. We can have ideas and thoughts in our heads all day long, but putting forth effort is what makes those ideas and goals real. And more importantly, achievable.

Make your reason bigger than you. Studies have shown it can take a person up to 10 weeks to form a new habit. Up until now, you have been habitually just eating. You don't know what you're eating. You don't know how many calories you're eating. You just eat and hope you are doing what you need to be doing. You think that if you eat healthy and don't track your foods, you will still reach your goals. You begin to wonder why, two years later, you have seen some progress, but aren't sure why you haven't been able to get over that plateau you've found yourself in. You begin to lose motivation. You begin to go back to the same old habits you had before. You then find yourself right back where you started.

2) PLAN AHEAD

The same as exercising, tracking your food first thing in the morning or the night before is going to be way more beneficial than trying to recall everything you ate at the end of the day. Does this mean you have to eat everything exactly as you planned it? No. It is just a whole lot less time consuming to change up a snack or meal you ate and may not have planned than it is to try and remember everything. I do this all the time. Maybe I planned out what I thought I was going to eat, but something came up and I had to substitute a meal replacement bar for lunch. While the food I planned may have been what I needed and the bar may have me adjusting the rest of my meals for that day, it doesn't have to mean you change everything.

Adjusting is way easier than trying to recall your entire day. Most of us are busy and running around all day. Think about the disservice you are doing if you don't plan ahead. Not only that, but if you know you have a busy day the following day, planning your meals beforehand will help you pack them up the following morning and/or get them ready the night before. Knowing ahead of time what you plan to eat not only helps you with time, but it also helps keep you on track. Having your meals available to you on a regular basis and having your goals written all over the place, will keep you on track and eventually, you will just stick to it because it makes everything more routine.

3) BE HONEST WITH YOURSELF

Maybe you got off your plan and you went way over on your calories and didn't hit your macronutrients for that day. Are you going to be honest with yourself and track it anyway or are you going to pretend it didn't happen? I have news for you – pretending it didn't happen isn't taking ownership. You have to take ownership of yourself. You have to hold yourself accountable. Again, go back to why you started doing this. Let that be what keeps you on track. We all have those days where maybe we ate something we know we shouldn't have. TRACK IT ANYWAY! I have good news for you – if you are trying to lose weight and you still burned more calories than you took in, that one meal isn't going to sabotage everything for you. The fact you still were honest with yourself and tracked it anyway is what is going to help you establish a new habit. If you don't put that meal in your food diary, who are you really hurting? Your friends? Your coach? NO! You are hurting yourself. You end up falling into this downward spiral, where you just say, "well, this meal won't hurt me since I already messed up." Then you just continue making excuses for your setback and continuing on a path of destruction. Don't let that happen to you. Remember again why you are doing this. Everything along the way boils down to your why.

4) HAVE A BACKUP PLAN

Maybe you didn't plan ahead. Maybe you are someplace and don't get service on your phone. Have a backup. Have a notebook on you at all times or take pictures of your meals. While it is always best to measure for accuracy, loose tracking is better than no tracking. Most restaurants menus are listed in the MyFitnessPal app. Even if you have to go back later and input the meal you ate, having a picture of it to remind you is a whole lot better than trying to remember off the top of your head. Always always ALWAYS have a backup plan. Life happens. It's not going to be perfect. You will have things come up and sometimes you will feel like life is just trying to go against you. That is far from the truth. You are in control here. If you have a backup plan, you are more likely to enter those foods into your diary. This creates what you need ultimately – consistency (step 6).

5) SET REMINDERS

New to diary tracking? Set reminders in your phone to go off each morning first thing. Wake up a little earlier so you make this portion of goal achievement priority. Don't place it on the backburner. Forgetting about it doesn't make it a reality. Doing it is what gets results. Once you see the reminder, do it right then. Don't wait. You have to want it more than you want anything else. You have to remember you are doing this for you and no one else. If you don't make it a priority, no one else will make it a priority for you.

6) MAKE IT A ROUTINE

Tracking your food doesn't have to be difficult. Just like anything else in life, the more you do it, the better you get. We all have "more important things" going on in our lives. But shouldn't our health be our priority over work or anything else? Think about step number one and what I said in step five. Every morning, first thing, make sure you are putting some time and effort into you. This means sitting down and really looking at your reasons behind why you are keeping a food diary and why this is important to you. This will keep you from veering if your reasons are deep enough for you.

Tracking your foods sometimes won't get you where you want to be in a short timeframe. Consistency matters. You need to make this part of your everyday routine. Otherwise, you will be months into doing this, and wonder why it isn't working.

Are you going to perfect right out the gate? Not at all! If you are just starting out and you forget a day, just don't forget the next day. We can never go back in time, but we can always move forward. One step in front of the other. You have to walk before you run. No one wakes up being amazing at something right off the bat. They may have natural talent, but in order to capitalize on that talent, they have to practice. If this is all new to you, it will take practice. Nevertheless, as long as you're willing to continue, you will get better, and eventually, it will all be second-nature.

7) NUTRITION FIRST

If you have to make a choice between tracking your food and going to the gym, choose nutrition first every time! I don't know how many times I have had to do this. I've had so many people, and I am one of them, come to me and say, "I work out, but I'm not seeing results." The first thing I ask them is if they know what they are eating. Usually I get a weird look. Most people think they are eating to their needs, but how do they really know? It's not always about losing inches and weight. How do you know if you are properly fueling your body if you aren't trying to keep track of it on a daily basis? Unless you eat the same EXACT foods every day, you should be tracking your food intake every day. Otherwise, the results will come a whole lot slower.

I struggled with this for quite some time. We all have those days where we just get busy and forget to track. My challenge to you is to use an alternate method, such as what I wrote about in Step 4.

I have literally had to skip the gym before to ensure my nutrition is complete for the day. Is it what I wanted to do? Of course not. BUT I knew it was more important to get my food in order. I can still do a quick 20-30-minute workout and expend some calories and allow myself to feel better. Nutrition has to be the priority though. Most of the studies you will find say that 80% of goal achievement in reaching a total health lifestyle comes from nutrition. I truly believe the percentage is higher. If you are lacking in this area, I have news for you – your workouts aren't helping you toward your goals as much as they could be.

It's time to stop the vicious cycle. It's time to stop making excuses. It's time to start realizing we are human and this is not something we are used to doing. It will be scary. You will make mistakes. However, if you keep just putting one foot in front of the other, before you know it, you will start reaching your milestones one by one. Eventually, you will reach your goals. Then, you make more goals so you continue the process. The journey is endless. It won't happen overnight. Be honest with yourself. Make this a priority in your life. Then each day, pat yourself on the back because guess what? You did it! You made the effort. You are already ahead of everyone out there who is still wishing and making excuses.

I noticed the same thing in my own life. Exercise and nutrition go hand and hand. When you eat better, you feel better. In return, you exercise. When you exercise, you eat better. You want to reach those goals. You want to fuel your body properly, if you care that is. Some people don't care. They just work out to work out or their goals only involve lifting weights heavier. The problem with this mindset is that they need to learn how to properly fuel their bodies so they can perform even better. There has to be a paired marriage between the two in order for a total health outcome to surface.

There are websites available to help you get started in learning more about Basal Metabolic Rate (BMR). There are also websites that tell you how to calculate your own macronutrients and calories. You can see more information in the worksheets located in the back of this book. I do advise anyone who wants to get started in learning how to eat to consult a trained professional who specializes in nutrition so that you are sure to get the correct information and do not become overwhelmed. A great app to use is called My Fitness Pal. However, I do advise having a trained professional to assist you with your numbers because the app is often not quite correct when it comes to that. Nevertheless, the app is a great tool to use when it comes to tracking food. It has a barcode scanner I absolutely love (even scanned the Japanese food when we were located in Okinawa, Japan) and it has a huge database of food so you aren't having to play the guessing game.

4.4 Intermittent Fasting

When I first became introduced to intermittent fasting, I was not a fan. I mean, I was telling people they needed to eat and now I am telling them to only eat in certain timeframes? Nevertheless, just like everything else, once I researched this more and realized just how beneficial it is to weight loss and especially for women and weight loss, I became more interested – there's that word again – interested. Let's look at fasting first.

I remember many years ago, when I would dabble in church (I say dabble because back then I thought just going was enough – boy, was I wrong!), I would hear the pastors talk about "fasting." Me, being the nutrition "expert" (or so I thought back then) did not agree with fasting. What is fasting? According to Merriam-Webster, *fast* in this sense means "to abstain from food or to eat sparingly or abstain from *some* foods. The reason I put the word "some" in italics was to show that it doesn't necessarily mean you have to take *everything* away. This is what I thought at first, especially as a new Christian. It's taking away *some* things in order to allow new things to come in and develop new habits. This is an important concept to remember as we continue going into this portion of the chapter.

Intermittent fasting just simply means we eat during a certain timeframe and fast during a certain timeframe. Let me be clear, this does *not* mean you get to eat anything and everything in sight during the eating time. We still have to make choices that will nourish our bodies.

Why does this concept work? For one thing, if you are someone who tends to overindulge all hours of the day and night, this will be an easier way to keep your cravings under control. The way you set up your schedule is by seeing what time you wake up and what time you normally go to bed first. Then you figure out what times of the day you are more active. This is when you want to fuel your body. For instance, I normally wake up super early. However, I may fast until a later time. I actually got to a point where I didn't have to eat before I worked out. This allows my body to use the energy that was stored from the day before. I burn more calories because my body is now turning what I have left over into what it needs to get me through my workout. With that said, I need to ensure I refuel after my workout. Therefore, my "fed state," or the time where I eat, may start around 5:30am. If you don't wake up until 7 or 7:30am, you can tweak your fed state and fasting state to meet your own needs. Maybe you go to work at 8am. You can have your first meal (maybe a healthy shake) before you go to work and allow your window to be twelve hours. The easiest way to determine your windows is to use the 12-hour rule. Feed for twelve hours and fast for twelve hours. My feeding window is about 14 hours now and my fasting state is about ten hours, which works for me. It allows me to continue fueling my body as needed throughout the day. This is where you have to figure out what works for *you*. Always remember this: what works for one person isn't going to work for everyone. Even if you are doing intermittent fasting, you still have to know how much food you need to intake each day. Therefore, you still need to know your BMR and activity level. Remember this as you continue.

Intermittent fasting is not necessarily an alternative to diary tracking. It is merely a way to help your metabolism get back on track. For women, this is important, since our bodies are genetically designed to hold on to body fat. We have a hormone called leptin, which is known as the "fat-burning hormone." Females have twice as much of this hormone than men; however, since we are child-bearing creatures, our bodies hold onto it to preserve the fat we have. So how do we get around this?

A couple years ago (2017), I began researching this more in-depth. Here is what I learned:

Leptin is a hormone that controls 100% of women's body's ability to burn fat. While we (females) have twice as much of this hormone than men, our bodies are far less responsive. Some women have "leptin resistance," which leads to "cottage cheese fat" – the fat normally accumulates in areas such as the hip/glute area and abdominal area in women.

For all of you "dieters" out there, this is the part that is going to help you understand why you should not sustain food intake lower than your BMR for a long period of time. This actually will cause your body to hold onto the fat in the long run and your temporary weight loss journey will lead you right back where you started. "When dieting, leptin levels drop significantly causing slow metabolism." This is why weight loss plateaus occur. People become impatient. They want to lose more weight in less time. They begin to restrict themselves and take diet pills that doctors give them to "suppress their appetite." I truly hate hearing this, because what tends to happen is the person taking the pills is doing more harm to their metabolism and body in the long run. Studies show that constantly dieting, not refueling the body properly, leads to weight gain instead of weight loss. Diet off, leptin levels low, fat piles back on after dieting (once you stop the diet, you've already made your leptin levels go low, that is why the weight just piles back on quickly).

Now do you see why I am not a fan of diets? Restrictive diets actually *hurt* the body's response to leptin. Women are genetically predisposed to being overweight. This is how God made us. It's up to us to form new habits that allow us to tap into the fat stores and ensure we are doing everything in our power to change the habits that have led us to where we are now. God also gave us science. He has allowed people to use their gifts and empowered them to learn more and run studies to enhance our thinking and give us more wisdom. Therefore, it is up to us to use wisdom to our benefit.

If you are a woman reading this, have you ever wondered why it is so much harder to lose weight after having a baby? Leptin levels following pregnancy drop significantly because our bodies are now holding onto everything to give to our baby. Nevertheless, as many of us have found, breastfeeding helps bring our leptin levels back up. This is why women who breastfeed tend to lose weight faster than women who don't.

There are certain things you can do to help tap back into your leptin levels. You override your metabolism using the scientific research provided in this book by unleashing your fat-burning potential. This is where intermittent fasting comes into play.

According to the research, "a 12-hr overnight fast (can extend to 16 hours on days you're not as active either at night or in the morning)." As I stated above, your window will depend on your schedule. Your schedule won't be like my schedule and my schedule most likely won't be like yours. For anyone interested in intermittent fasting when working with me, I always ask about their schedule. This way I can help guide them and formulate a fed and fasting window for them to follow.

Another thing you should consider if you are a woman who is in a caloric deficit to lose weight: you can't stay in a caloric deficit for too long. You need to refeed at least once every 5-6 days. If you are in a caloric deficit during the week, maybe one day on the weekend, you should go back to your maintenance levels. This is another reason why having someone who specializes in this area is helpful when starting out.

I began doing my research on leptin more as I learned how to lean down for bodybuilding shows. Knowing how to properly utilize intermittent fasting and how to properly refuel was key to my success in 2018. I used nutrition to get where I needed to be for the stage. I had a couple injuries that kept me from exercising too much, so I really had to dig deep and rely on the research I had done, tracking my food, and using the science to lean out naturally. Not only did I look better that year than I had in previous years listening to others who were not using science, but I also felt better the day of the show and I placed better than I had before. All around, I felt good knowing I had used the knowledge gained through sheer passion and interest to reach my goals. I am now using that same knowledge to help others reach their goals. It's not rocket science, but it is a science.

There is a phenomena called "ego depletion," which pertains to the following: throughout the day, your reserve of mental and emotional energy becomes depleted and your ability to resist temptation gets weaker, hence "ego DEPLETION." I've found that it's easiest to cut back on food and avoid cravings and temptations earlier in the day because your willpower and ego reserve is highest. Toward the end of the day, when your reserve of willpower is drained from the stresses of daily life, you become less capable of resisting temptation. This is when people say they "binge eat."

Many women have found it better to save more of their calories towards the end of the day when cravings start occurring. However, if you do not have cravings later in the day, this isn't necessary. It all depends on when you are most active. The main point is staying within your caloric and macro needs. You also want to fuel your body around the times you are most active. If you are like me and wake up early, you are most likely more active towards the beginning of the day. You need to fuel your body earlier in order to be able to perform better in your field and in all your obligations. As the day goes by, you can begin to cut back on food and make sure you are drinking more water. Sometimes, when our brain triggers hunger, it is really because we are thirsty. When the cravings occur, try drinking a glass of water. Put your mind on something else, and see what happens. You may be able to change those habits of grabbing food first thing, which will lead to better results in the long run.

When it comes to food, it is vital to know what type of allergies or sensitivities you have. Sometimes, you will want to see a registered dietician who has a body scan. He or she will be able to tell you through that scan if there are some underlying conditions that are keeping you from seeing results. For instance, you need to find out is if you have soy sensitivity. If you take in high levels of soy, your body may not be able to process it well. An easy fix to this is simply by lowering the amount of soy you ingest and see how your body reacts.

When I talk to people about their nutrition, I often listen to what they say about their current trials and I also ask about what they have tried in the past. I have them fill out a questionnaire. This way, I can see if they have done any internal damage and help them get their bodies back to where it needs to be for optimal performance and success in the area of weight loss (or gaining muscle). It also allows me to be able to counsel them better if they are someone who has tried every diet out there and has rebounded each time. More time has to be taken to find underlying triggers that keeps them on these diets and holds them captive in eating disorders. As their coach, it is important for me to have this information. This way, I can guide them better and make sure I am there with them when they need me the most.

If you have further questions about intermittent fasting, diary tracking, BMR, calorie tracking, and/or diary tracking, please feel free to contact me directly. I would love to assist you on your journey.

4.5 Science Over Fads

"Keep us from being tempted and protect us from evil."
– Matthew 6:13

Yep, I said it. NO FAD DIETS! I've said it a few times already, but it is a point I intend to make clear in this chapter: for many reasons (some already listed), I am NOT an advocate of diets. I am not one who says, "stay away from 'bad food.'" I don't like to call it "bad," because if you put that type of label on it, research has shown it could potentially make you feel "bad" about yourself if you eat it. Therefore, we do not want to put any negative connotations on foods. We do want to "choose healthier choices" when we can and portion our food. We also want to make sure we are eating enough and eating around the most active parts of our days. I will not tell you that you shouldn't go out to eat. I will not tell you that you have to cut your calories to an extreme amount or cut a certain macronutrient (often people cut carbs because they heard it works – but they don't do the proper research to find out why and how it works, so they end up harming themselves internally more than helping themselves). Why won't I tell you to do these things? First, I feel as if anything that has the word "diet" in it, is temporary. It most likely is NOT something you will do for the rest of your life. If that is the case, what is the point in doing it? Also, if you go out with friends and family, I want you to simply have better habits, so you can make healthier choices that will serve your body and brain better.

This is a statement I hear a lot:

"Well, it must work because I am losing weight or [insert name here] lost weight."

It does work ... temporarily ... until you begin adding those foods back in and gaining the weight right back.

In every fad out there, the first question I always ask someone who is partaking is if it is something they are going to do for the rest of their life. If the answer is no, I ask them why they are wasting their time on it now. Most of the time, they say they just want to lose a certain amount of weight and then they will go back to what they were doing before. The problem with that is, unless they are someone who specializes in nutrition, the likelihood of not gaining the weight back once they finish their fad nutrition plan is slim to none. Why not allow someone who does specialize in nutrition guide you on your journey?

I used to be pretty stubborn when it came to a lot of things, so I never judge anyone. They are going to do what they want to do until they learn otherwise that it may not be the best overall option. Most people just have to learn on their own. I never try to push anyone to using science. All I say is that science is what works. Ask anyone who has tried everything else under the sun.

Ok, sure, you do your 21 Day Fix and lose some weight, get the body you've been wanting, and then the 21 days is over. Now what? You're probably splurging because you have been depriving yourself. And then, what's more? You end up gaining that weight right back. All that deprivation and the system you did for that small amount of time got you right back to square one. Why? Well, for one, you did not develop any real habits. You committed for a short period of time, but you didn't truly learn HOW to eat and WHAT your body needs. So how does that help you for the long term? Well, simply stated, it doesn't.

I am an advocate for learning how to eat for the rest of your life. If you are one of those who can be on a Keto Diet for the rest of your life and you feel good about it, I am happy for you. I will not try to deter you from that lifestyle because you have made it just that – a lifestyle. However, what I have seen more of, is people will try something for a little while and then they want to go back to what they were doing before, which wasn't working either. So again, they are back to square one. They didn't learn how to eat. They didn't learn how to properly nourish their bodies. They learned how to follow a plan for a limited amount of time.

Take my client, Regina. Regina and I started working together over three years ago. At the time, I was a personal trainer at a local gym. She heard about me and after our consultation, decided she wanted to work with me. While I was training her, I would educate her on certain things, especially form and positioning. She was a fast learner and we worked on a lot of core and lower body movements (I do that a lot with my clients because most of them have weaker core stability). As we continued to work together, I wanted to do more with Regina's nutrition. We worked on that aspect of things for quite some time. She had tried every "diet" in the book and was very skeptical when I had her eating more. She wanted to be in a caloric deficit. At first, it worked. However, she saw first-hand what happens when women are in a calorie deficit for too long (as mentioned above).

As we continued, and I learned more and more about ways to alter the human body's natural response to certain stimuli (and how to use leptin to our advantage as women), I continued to provide Regina (and many others) with the tools that would help her. As I learn, I share. Once Regina shifted her mindset around food, she began to see the results she desired. She began to love herself and love food. She built a different relationship with food and allowed it to help her instead of hindering her in her goals.

The thing about science is that new case studies are coming out all the time. Also, each person is different. What works for one person is not going to work best for someone else. Therefore, with each client, I had a new learning experience. That's what I really enjoy about it though. It never gets boring. I learned how to calculate macronutrients and calorie requirements over time. Regina asked me to calculate her requirements, so I did. By this time, I had gone through nutrition certifications and was learning more and more over time. I also have a medical laboratory technician background, so I also look at vitamin and mineral intake, as well as sugar and fiber intake. This is where my research on Juice Plus and 1st Phorm came into play. In researching and learning more about these companies, their products, and what they are about, I realized they were companies I wanted to be a part of. They allow me to help people in this area (nutrition) even more.

Check out the following websites for more on these products and offers:

https://1stphorm.com/jodionamission
http://jodiwatkins.juiceplus.com
http://jodiwatkins.towergarden.juiceplus.com

> *"After all, no one ever hated their own body, but they feed and care for their body, just as Christ does the church."*
> - Ephesians 5:29

One thing I have never heard anyone say is they are not willing to take care of themselves. Most of us don't even realize the toxins we are putting into our bodies. I was there, believe me. However, once I began learning about foods, tracking them, and seeing what I was doing, my eyes opened and I knew I wasn't doing what I needed to do in order to live healthier, more fulfilled lives. All it takes is being willing to make one small change at a time. Matthew 6:34 says, *"Therefore, do not worry about tomorrow, for tomorrow will worry about itself. Each day has enough trouble on its own."* I think what gets us all when we are implementing something new into our lives is the fear of failure. We don't want to start because we are afraid we are going to fail. This mindset keeps us from being able to accomplish anything. My advice is to begin where you are. Don't worry about the outcome. Just begin. That way, you aren't worried about failing. It doesn't even register into your mind. You are simply taking the first step and learning how to do things a little differently than you have before.

Nutrition is the most important part of becoming healthier. It's not only important to know about calories and macronutrients, but also about the vitamins and minerals you are getting each day. Vitamins and minerals help keep our immune systems strong and allow us to have the energy we need to get through the day. Don't forget about the water. Make it fun. Use a gallon jug holder like the one found at the company, Gallon Gear (www.gallongear.com). It's a great conversation starter and could serve as your purse if you're like me. Use code "JodiW" at checkout to get 15% off.

It's also good to learn about proper sugar and fiber intake and how to make those things useful in getting healthier. Natural sugars are always better for you than processed sugars and sugar alcohols (aka, fake sugar).

Need more assistance and education in this area? Contact me and I will help you get on the right track. I love educating others on this subject and how proper nutrition affects our bodies on so many levels. I have a team of passionate nutrition specialists who also want to help you in this area. All you have to do is reach out. We are here for you.

This chapter could easily be a book in itself. The important thing to remember is that when it comes to self-care, having a good relationship with food is truly important. Nutrition is key. It takes patience and the willingness to want to learn. There are no quick fixes when it comes to getting healthy. You have to remember why you started and always keep that in the back of your mind when you feel like quitting. What's better is while you are learning, you can also teach others and even share insight with your family so they are healthier as well. This is why learning how to eat is so much better than relying on meal replacements and fad (short-term) solutions to an often-long-term problem.

Don't get discouraged. Noah didn't build the ark in one day and you WILL eventually learn how to FULLY take care of yourself. You just have to be willing to trust the process, just as Regina finally did. Tracking your foods also doesn't have to be something you do for the rest of your life. Once you learn what your body needs and how to properly fulfill those needs, you begin to lay off tracking and rely on what you've learned. It's a great feeling and allows us to show up for those who count on us every day.

4.6 The Science and Why It Works

> *"The simple believe anything, but the prudent give thoughts to their steps."*
>
> – Proverbs 14:15

Don't believe everything. I surely didn't. I did my research and through experience and training in these areas, I can now bring my findings to you. I truly want you to succeed. I did all the legwork for you. I have given you all the tools. All you have to do now is try it yourself and see what you think. Remember that it takes time, but it has one thing that diets don't have – sustainability.

I said it above and I am going to say it again: it's not rocket science, it's health science. It's life. It's learning how to use research to help you reach your health and wellness goals. It's creating a lifestyle that allows you to be happy, while still working towards your goals.

Science works because our bodies are filled with complexities that allow it to function in a way we could never have made up. The Lord has made us to be these machines. However, if we do not treat our bodies as such, they will break down. They will begin to deteriorate. We will become sick. We will endure unfathomable pain. We will not allow the machines to perform as advertised.

When I meet people, who don't know how to take care of themselves, I now feel as though the Lord has *tasked* me to give them knowledge in these areas. Maybe they don't care. Maybe they don't *really* want to hear it at the time. I don't preach and I *don't* make anyone feel guilty. Why would I do that? I have been where they are! What I do now is provide *wisdom*.

It's simple. If you don't give your body the right fuel, it will break down. Then what? Most people don't want to practice preventative medicine.

Nevertheless, when they are lying in a hospital in pain and agony, they will most likely wish they had. Don't let it get to that. You have the power *right now* to change your outcome. It doesn't matter if you are already taking blood pressure medications. It doesn't matter if you are already diabetic. It doesn't matter if you have already developed a tumor the size of your fist. Until you take your last breath, it is **NOT** too late!

Therefore, I challenge you today to take a stand. Begin taking small steps towards a better outcome. Begin giving your body the nutrients and water it needs. All you have to do is be willing to *begin*. Once you begin, you keep going. You continue to take steps that will lead to a better you. A year from now, you may just be off those medications. You may be able to move better. You may not have those headaches that were causing debilitating pain and causing you to be bed-ridden all day. You may have more energy to get through the day. You may just be able to *live life* the way God always wants us *all* to live it. Change your mindset, be willing to change some habits, and see what happens when you continue making more changes and getting rid of the habits that were once holding you back. I look forward to hearing how it goes for you. I look forward to hearing your new outcome and your wins. This is where it begins. You want to take care of you. It goes back to the previous chapter – Self Care. Once you give yourself the ok to take care of you, amazing things will begin to happen.

Trust in the Lord and He will guide you. Don't lean on your own understanding. He has you. Lean on *Him* and let the rest become a part of your distant history!

> *"Trust in the Lord with all your heart and lean not on your own understanding; in all your ways submit to him, and he will make your paths straight. Do not be wise in your own eyes; fear the Lord and shun evil. This will bring health to your body and nourishment to your bones."*
>
> – Proverbs 3: 5-8

Chapter 5
Exercise

5.1 Love the Feeling of Becoming Energized

"Let us not become weary in doing good, for at the proper time we will reap a harvest if we do not give up."

- Galatians 6:9

Exercise is a key component to releasing endorphins, tapping into hormones that give you an amazing feeling. If it is not that for you, it is time to re-evaluate what you are doing. Otherwise, you will never enjoy it and will not be willing to make it a part of your daily habit. The one thing people do that can really deter them from continuing is trying to do too much too quickly. If you are not used to going to the gym or exercising regularly, saying you are going to do it six times per week is setting yourself up for failure. Start off with a more feasible goal: "I am going to strength train two times per week and walk for 30 minutes three times per week." This is a feasible goal and is not too much where you will begin to dread it. After a few weeks, you change things up a little by adding some intensity or maybe another strength workout. A program that implements three days of strength training is going to be valuable to your goals, especially if you are trying to lose weight. Many people think they have to lift weights six times per week. This is not true. The quality of your workout is more important than the quantity. Focusing on your meals and making sure you are staying within your nutrition goals is really what matters.

According to one source, "Regular physical activity has amazing benefits."

Here are just a few:

1. Physical activity helps you **live longer and prevent many chronic diseases,** such as heart disease, high blood pressure, abnormal blood lipid (cholesterol and triglyceride) profile, stroke, type 2 diabetes, metabolic syndrome, and colon and breast cancers.

2. Physical activity **improves cardio-respiratory and muscular fitness.**

3. Physical activity **raises your metabolism and helps you lose weight more easily** (or eat more without gaining weight).

4. Physical activity helps **reduce stress, anxiety, and depression and improve your mood.**

5. Physical activity helps **maintain brain function in older adults.**

6. Physical activity helps with **digestion and promotes regular bowel movements.**

7. Physical activity **increases bone density.**

8. Physical activity helps you **age more gracefully by maintaining your looks and your agility.**

9. Physical activity **improves sleep quality.**

10. Physical activity **improves your overall quality of life."**[12]

1 Corinthians 3:17 says, *"If anyone destroys God's temple, God will destroy that person; for God's temple is sacred, and you together are that temple."*

If God charges us to take care of His temple, why is it so difficult for us to do want to find answers so that we can truly do everything in our power to take care of these temples we have been given? I, too, took my temple for granted for many years. However, through a major occurrence in my life, I realized just how important it was to take care of this temple in all ways possible. I will never say I have total control. I have no idea where my life will take me or how long I have left on this earth. However, I *can* make it a point to do everything in my power to seek information that will help me take care of myself and combat things that *are* in my control.

Knowing the benefits of exercise should be enough to get people motivated. So why do we see so much obesity in the world today if exercise is so good for you? For one, people are so focused on the other pillars in this system. For one, they often tell themselves they can't. That is already setting them up for failure. They say things like, "I don't have time" or "I work too much" or "I have small children and can't get away." Then don't! Get your kids involved! Get the family involved. Having a negative mindset is what holds so many people back. We have to get past that part before any program we get into will be effective. We all have time for things that are important. Tell me again why your health is not important to you. That is basically what you are telling yourself when you say things out loud to make you feel better about putting off your commitments to yourself.

5.2 Have Balance Without Becoming Overwhelmed

> *"But those who hope in the Lord will renew their strength. They will soar on wings like eagles; they will run and not grow weary, they will walk and not be faint."*
>
> – Isaiah 40:31

Once you have worked on time management and setting your schedule, you can then begin to figure out when you can exercise and what types of exercises you need. Remember it's all about balance. You have to *find* time in your schedule and make sure it's something you can *commit* to. If you don't know where to start, it's ok to look for the answers in the right places.

I have some people who are not ready for an exercise program just yet. Maybe their doctor has not cleared them yet or they have an underlying condition that severely limits their abilities. We start slow. Maybe just going for a walk each day for 20 minutes is what they need to start out. I make sure to work closely with their doctor(s) and ensure I do not have them doing anything outside of what they need to do. Trainers have to operate within their scope of practice. Make sure your trainer is doing just that. Trainers are not there to diagnose. They are there to help. They are also there to teach you and maybe even push you past your own limits. A good trainer will empower you and ensure you are learning as much as you are doing. If you have a trainer who is not educating you during your sessions, you may want to look into hiring someone else. It should not just be about what they get from you, but really what you receive from them.

5.3 Being Wiser

> *"If any of you lack wisdom, you should ask God, who gives generously to all without finding fault, and it will be given to you."*
> – James 1:5

When you are beginning your journey, seek God first and He will bring you to the right people who will help you learn how to begin properly. Unfortunately, in this day and age, you can't rely on just anyone. Technology and the internet have made it possible for more people to receive a certification; however, the person has to go from there and begin learning more on their own through experience. If it's in God's plan, I hope to be able to mentor other personal trainers and use the knowledge the Lord has given to me to help them see just how important their job is to the people who seek assistance from them. As trainers, it is up to us to go above and beyond to learn as much as we can about our craft. It has to be a passion that is ignited and fueled the more we develop.

There are a lot of people out there who claim to know how to work out. Before you agree to work with someone, make sure you do your research. Ask questions. Be sure anyone you plan to hire has your best interests in mind. Do not just go for the cheapest price, or you may encounter subpar training from someone who is inexperienced. It happens all the time. If you need help learning how to exercise properly, it's important to work with someone who is trained. The Lord has provided us with brains. Therefore, it's important for you to use it and do your research. Find someone who has worked with people of different capabilities. What type of certifications do they have? Do they have any testimonials? What is their specialty? If you have an injury or chronic pain, you will want to find someone who has dealt with that before. You also want to make sure any professional you are working with – doctors, physical therapists, nutritionists, etc – are willing and able to work with your personal trainer to ensure you are being prescribed exercises that will help you become stronger without further injury.

I have personally had five major surgeries – three on one knee and one on each shoulder. I have had to start over A LOT! I have also been to physical therapy for different issues and learned how to recover properly. These are all tactics that I use in training myself and others. I am able to push the person who wants to compete in bodybuilding, but I am also able to digress and help people recover from injuries or learn how to exercise with existing pain and inflammation (arthritis or any of the other "-itis'." This is through the experience I have personally had. I am able to take what I have learned and help others learn as well. Not everyone can do that. So, make sure whoever you get to help you is truly there to help YOU ... not just fulfilling a slot or their own agenda. They have to want to put you first. Otherwise, you are wasting your time and your money.

Some people don't have a gym membership. What should they do? They don't need to have one. Normally, they can get a perfectly good workout at home with a few items and their body. However, some personal trainers in the gyms don't teach that. They don't all teach the people they are working with how to operate effectively on their own. I had a client last year who told me she used to have a trainer, but he would do everything for her. When it was time for her to do things on her own, she didn't remember what to do. What good is that? We, as trainers and coaches, should be empowering our clients so they can do more on their own. Otherwise, it becomes a flawed system. I guess it is job security knowing that person has to keep coming back to you, but I would rather allow that person to prosper over time, flee the nest, and bring me someone else I can mold over time to do the same. I love it when clients come back to me after a few years to let me know they are still doing the stuff we did together and they still remember to watch their form and how to optimize the exercises – slow and controlled, I always say.

You should not need someone to hold your hand all the time. Eventually, you have to be able to operate on your own in order to be able to sustain it over a long period of time. This is why it baffles me when people tell me they "need" face-to-face training and that online training isn't for them. They "need" someone there to push them. In reality, they just need to get over themselves and focus on the goal. This is why I put exercise as the fifth step in my system. It takes getting over your mindset, learning time management, learning that it's ok to take some time for yourself, and learning how to use food as your main source of energy and fuel, before you can effectively execute a workout program. Nevertheless, most people do not want to hear this.

Countless times, people have told me they love to workout and exercise, but they don't want to go on a diet. Who does? This is why I don't do diets. You learn HOW to eat. Otherwise, your workouts are going to be about 90% less effective. A combination of learning proper nutrition AND getting a customized workout program you can do literally anywhere on YOUR time is a winning combination by far.

5.4 Why Strength Training is Important/Dispelling the Myths

> *"They will turn their ears away from truth and turn aside to myths"*
>
> - 2 Timothy 4:4

Most women are quick to begin a cardiovascular exercise program, and that is awesome, especially for those who are just starting out. Anything is better than nothing all day long. However, learning how to lift weights has benefits for women especially that most are not aware of. Want to lose body fat quickly? Implementing regular strength training into your routine is one of the quickest ways to lose body fat (along with proper fuel intake of course). Women, on average, store at least 10% more body fat than men. That means it's more difficult for us to lose body fat. However, it isn't impossible. Implement a balance of cardio and strength training and see what happens. You may be surprised. MYTH BUSTER: You are *not* going to get "bulky" if you lift weights. Did you know that most of the muscular women you see have that muscle because they worked *really* hard to get it? Maybe it was through nutrition (eating a lot more than we burn to develop the muscle and eating a lot of protein, which is not what most of the women in the world do ... so just lifting weights doesn't give you more muscle than you want. There are other things involved in that portion of it all). What lifting weights *will* do is allow you to feel more confident and be stronger. Burn more calories *all day long* with strength training.

One study found that "regular strength training can increase your RMR - Resting Metabolic Rate - by about 5%. This means your body burns more calories throughout the day - even while you're NOT working out. The higher your RMR, the faster you burn fat, and the quicker you lose weight."[15] Strength training in women decreases the likelihood of developing osteoporosis. Strength training has been proven to increase bone density, which in turn, decreases the development of osteoporosis (loss of bone density). One other thing strength training does is helps reduce the risk of heart disease. If you have any form of heart disease in your family, I highly recommend adding a good strength training program into your routine. Cardiovascular exercise is great, and strength training doesn't have to be done every day, but a balance of both along with proper nutrition is the best way to reach your overall health and wellness goals!

5.5. Creating an Action Plan

> *"Dear children, let us not love with words or speech but with actions and in truth."*
>
> — 1 John 3:18

One thing I always tell those who I work with is this: I can give you all the tools I have ever learned in my entire life – everything God has given me to share – but if you are not willing to use them, they become nothing. This is something I have also learned about God's word. He provides all the wisdom we need. However, if we are not willing to use the words to our benefit, we become lost and we end up relying on ourselves and other humans to get us where we need to be. It starts with renewal of the mind. Once we trust the Lord with all our hearts, we can believe He will direct us to the people who will work through Him to help us in areas such as health and wellness. Maybe, if the Lord feels I am a good fit for you, He will lead you to me. If you are reading this book, maybe He has already done that for you. As I continue my journey in trusting in Him to guide me, He sends me those people who He knows I will take care of. I am not in control of who He sends me. He knows I am not for everyone and everyone is not for me. However, there are people out there who He knows I can and will take care of. Those are the people He guides to work with me more in-depth.

Remember that not every day will be a great day. You will have days where you have to force yourself to get going. However, take it from me, those are the days where you need to exercise even more. You will feel so much better. Otherwise, you may go through the day blaming yourself and just having a bad day all around.

Let's talk about how to build your exercise schedule. I often get asked, "when is the best time to work out?"

No matter what the research says, the absolute BEST time to exercise is the time that you will stick to. It's the time you are going to keep your promises to yourself and stay consistent. For me, first thing in the morning or at least earlier in the day is best. Besides all the scientific reasons for why workout earlier in the day is beneficial, a reason it works for me is because I can't predict what is going to happen in the rest of the day. When "life happens," it will not have a negative effect on the outcome of your goal. It starts my day on a positive note and allows me to be more productive. It just works for me.

Many people say they would rather wait until "after work." This never worked for me because there were times I had to work late. As a parent, I have encountered times where my child became sick at school and I had to pick her up. Not only that, but it seems to be easier to talk to yourself out of doing it as time goes by during the day – just a fact. There are just so many things that are out of our control. In my opinion and from what I have learned in my own life, getting your exercise first thing in the morning will free you from being held back later in the day. Besides, after a long day of work, who wants to work out still?

When something becomes important to us, we have to make it a priority. Mark 1:35 says, *"Very early in the morning, while it was still dark, Jesus got up, left the house and went off to a solitary place, where he prayed."* Even though I had not worked on my faith until more recently, my praying time was going to the gym. I went before anyone was up. I went before most people, so it wouldn't be too busy. I made it a priority. As I got further into my spiritual journey, I used this same concept when it came to reading the Word and praying. Now, I wake up and give some time to the Lord first and foremost. Then, on the days I have planned to go to the gym, I go before anything else can get in the way. I follow the path Jesus already laid out. The Lord already told us the best time to do things we aren't used to doing and that should be most important to us. It is written. All we have to do is follow what it says.

Many of those who plan to exercise after a full day or work or other obligations are unable to stay consistent. They quit because it becomes too difficult to stick to the schedule they created as they leaned on what *they* thought was best. When we attempt to rely on ourselves, we are actually setting ourselves up for failure.

Not a morning person? Neither was I. Jesus probably wasn't either when He was a baby. He had to grow into it, just as we do. All you have to do is begin creating a new ritual. Start out by waking up a mere 15 minutes earlier. Make it a priority and put it into action. Don't just "say" you're going to do it. Start with 15 minutes and go from there. Eventually, you will have yourself on a good schedule and life won't be able to get in the way of your goals, for the most part. Will it be perfect? No. Maybe you aren't able to get to bed as early one night or you wake up not feeling well. There are certain things that will be out of your control. Lean on what the Lord has already written for us and it will guide you into your new journey. He will guide you. All you have to do is be obedient and walk in pure faith. He will give you grace the more you continue on your journey, just as He has given to me.

Your schedule will make or break you. Not putting you first in the day will keep you from being successful throughout the rest of the day when it comes to dealing with people and situations that will try to keep you from your goals. Anyone who is a believer can tell you the more you try to do better for yourself and listen to God's word, the more the enemy will come in and do everything He can to pull you back to where you are. The enemy wants you to be comfortable. The enemy does *not* want you to progress. He doesn't want you to transform. It is up to *you* to ensure the enemy can *not* take you down once you begin this journey.

Find the time that works for you. Schedule it just as you would a doctor appointment and don't cancel it. Become unavailable at that time. Do whatever you have to do to begin. Once you begin and form the habit, it will be even easier not to quit or blow it off. Therefore, if you say you are going to work out at noon every day, work out at noon. If your schedule changes at work or with other obligations, still factor in your "Me" time. Otherwise, one day missed will turn into two, two will turn into three, three will turn into a week, and so on. You will be right back where you started. If you need a plan and some accountability, that's where a good certified personal trainer/coach comes into play. Make sure it is someone who knows what they are doing and has your best interest in mind. That way, you won't dread your sessions, but you'll enjoy them enough to see progress and want to keep going. It's also great to invite someone to come along with you. That way, even on the days you don't necessarily feel like going, you will still go because you know there is someone else holding you accountable. Just make sure it is someone who is motivated as well. Otherwise, you will both end up skipping the day, which will lead to two, then three, and so on. Those are NOT the accountability partners you want in any area of life. Have someone who is going to push you as much or more as you push them. Make a schedule and keep to it. Define your goal and figure out the days you are going to keep your promise to yourself. Write it down in your schedule. Make it a priority. Also, have options for home workouts if you are not able to get to the gym. Exercise is important. Incorporate it in more for how it makes you feel and as you begin to enjoy it, you will be able to continue. It doesn't even have to be going to the gym. It could be something you do with your family. Make it fun and remember it shouldn't be something extra. It should be a lifestyle, just like everything else we have talked about in this book.

Begin by making a *commitment* to yourself.

Step 1: Commit. Write down the days of the week (I recommend three days for beginners) you are going to commit time to exercise. Keep your calendar where you can see it.

Step 2: Prepare. The night before, have your clothes laid out and shoes ready to go. This way, you aren't making excuses or wasting time when you are getting ready to go. This also goes for food and water. Make sure you have everything you need to ensure your success.

Which days will you commit to in the next six weeks? Check your schedule, then use this space to write it down. Use a calendar and set reminders so you aren't as willing to blow it off. Make it important.

Days of the Week I Will Commit to in the Next Six Weeks (If just starting out, pick 3; if more advanced, pick 4-5, but make sure you give your body time to rest and recover as well):

Sunday

Monday

Tuesday

Wednesday

Thursday

Friday

Saturday

Which time of the day is more feasible for me (be honest here – think about your obligations first and where you can *promise* yourself this time?

Morning

Afternoon

Evening

Looking at my schedule for this week, I will commit to the following times for the days I have chosen (if you have 4 or 5 days, write it down in a separate notebook, commit it to your schedule, and do it!):

Day 1 –

Day 2 –

Day 3 –

My promise to myself: On the days I commit to exercise, I will do everything in my power not to break that promise. Whether I am just going for a walk or going to the gym, I have made this time available for my health and wellness journey. I am going to keep this promise because if I let myself down, I will regret it. I will also have no one else to blame. God wants me to be healthy, so He tasks me to do what it takes in order to make that happen.

Say the above statement to yourself and remember this is your journey. While you may invite others to join, the choice to actually do everything you have learned up to now is ultimately yours. You are not in competition with anyone else. You are NOT perfect. If you have to miss one of your chosen days due to unforeseen circumstances, keep track of those circumstances and make sure you exercise another day so that you still keep your original promise to yourself.

You can do this! If you need assistance with customized workout programs, please contact me. I would love to be a part of your journey. Don't let your life pass you by without making it a point to implement exercise into your life. You may be surprised when you actually *enjoy* it and *need* it. Just wait.

Chapter 6
Forming Habits Through Consistency

6.1 Repeat and Practice

> *"Whatever you have learned or received or heard from me, or seen in me - put into practice. And the God of peace will be with you."*
> – Philippians 4:9

Practice means doing something repeatedly until it becomes a habit. Practice does not mean quitting something a few days after trying it. Think about something you are currently good at. How did you become good at it? My guess is you continuously practiced until it became second-nature.

Take exercise for example. Do you think everyone just woke up knowing how to properly workout? Not at all. It took education in most cases, research of some sort, and putting it all into play through practice.

Have you ever played sports? If so, you know all about practice. As a basketball player in my earlier days, I spent hours "practicing." I would practice my weaknesses in order to make them strengths. While that was not the path God had for me as a career, it was something I was passionate about when I was younger. I wanted to learn the game. I wanted to learn how to become better. In anything I do in my life now, I always go back to that. If it is something I want to be better at doing,

I learn it and I put it into practice. I first learned how to strength train when I was practicing with the basketball team at Santa Fe Community College in Gainesville, FL back in 1996/97. I was a scrawny kid who needed to gain muscle and become stronger in order to have any chance of being an asset to the team. The athletic trainer there began teaching me how to use the machines. I really enjoyed learning and challenging my body in a whole new way. I was 18 at the time and had never learned up to that point how to strength train. In high school, I played basketball and ran track. However, we never had machines to use and didn't have anyone to teach us. It was a smaller school in a smaller town. I was just happy to have an amazing mentor and coach to help me get through some tough times and be there to continue supporting and believing in me. Lifting weights wasn't even a thought in my head.

As time went on, I continued to use the machines at Santa Fe. Later on, toward the end of 1997 (I was 19 by this time), I began working at a renowned health and fitness center in Gainesville which still stands to this day. Gainesville Health and Fitness has really changed the game for fitness centers all over the world. Even back then, it was a prestigious two-story facility with an indoor basketball court (which I loved of course), machines galore, and an upper room with free weights (which I never really used back then due to lack of knowledge). My reasons for working at this facility were simply because I was a college student who had accumulated a lot of debt and could not afford the membership fee. I was using a guest pass and on the final day when they wanted me to join as a member, I simply asked if they were hiring. At the time, I was working towards my Associates of Science degree in Sports and Exercise Science. Therefore, they hired me to be someone who greeted and assisted members.

As a bonus, I received a free membership: win-win. As I went through the orientation, myself and the other new hires learned there would be a series of interviews. We weren't quite hired just yet. We had to pass the interviews in order to be considered. One of the interviews was a workout interview, where the person in charge had the job to put us through one of the most rigorous workouts to the point where we wanted to basically throw up. They warned us not to eat right before coming for this interview. I have always been pretty competitive as far back as I remember and there was no way I wasn't going to make it through this portion of the interview process.

While the workout was the most strenuous workout I'd ever encountered, it really lit a passion inside me to learn even more. That began my journey in strength training. However, life happened – a lot of life – and I did not continue that journey until after I joined the military. Even then, I would dabble, but I was not on a consistent schedule. Nevertheless, I would say this was my "practice time." I never completely stopped. However, I stayed where I was comfortable. I used the machines I was comfortable using. It wasn't until 2013 (and after I received my personal trainer certification) that I finally made it important to learn more about proper lifting and nutrition.

As you can see, my journey did NOT happen overnight. I did not wake up knowing what to do. It was a long process. It took a whole lot of practice and it took me wanting to learn. I also wanted to ensure I was doing everything in my power to become healthier. I learned how to exercise properly and I learned how to fuel my body with proper nutrients and calories. I learned how to alter my body however I needed to for bodybuilding. Nevertheless, I had to have two things: the willingness to be patient and not allow my pride to get in the way and the willingness to practice the craft, just as I did with basketball and track growing up.

6.2 Tell Your Story

Something I am learning now that I wish I had known many years ago, is the best way to heal or overcome a setback, is to write a story about it. Share it with the rest of the world. Become transparent. Be vulnerable. Don't worry about what others think of you. Just tell the story. When I first had the idea for this book, I asked other women if they would like to contribute. My good friend, Jamie Johnson, reached out and has an amazing story of strength and consistency. This story also exemplifies how important it is to have an accountability partner when you are first starting out. Jamie could have never shown up when the lady who offered to help her told her to meet her early in the morning.

It's a choice we all have. She could have continued down the same rabbit hole she was already going down. Nevertheless, she let go of her pride and allowed herself to become vulnerable and be encouraged. Jamie and I both grew up in Fernandina Beach, Florida. We learned a lot about life back then. However, nothing would prepare us for our future. We both have experienced pain. We also now get to experience healing through sharing our stories to encourage others. Let's take a look at Jamie's health story.

> I am Jamie Johnson and I would like to tell my story. I grew up in a small town in Florida known as O'Neil (Fernandina Beach). This was known as the country. I grew up eating fresh fruit, vegetables that my grandparents and parents grew in their gardens and meats that were raised by them as well. As a kid I was quite small and actually had to gain weight to join the military. I left for the Air Force in 1997 at the age of 19. However, like most people I did a lot of damage to myself in my 20s and early 30's eating unhealthy foods, drinking and thinking I was invincible. I could party and drink with the best of them and still could pass my fitness tests. I was 5'1, 120 with a 28 inch waist. Having a small waist helped me to my advantage because I could pass my test with waist alone. I wasn't very athletic as far as running was concerned so I only would run when it was a month before my annual fitness test. As the years passed, I went from passing my fitness tests to barely passing the new Air Force fitness standards.
>
> In 2005, I fell while running my fitness test. Unbeknownst to me I had chipped my knee cap and tore my meniscus. I constantly had knee pain and during this time was when I started to gain weight. I also found out I was having problems with my thyroid which made it even harder for me to lose weight. From 2006 until 2011, my weight fluctuated and I got bigger after my 2nd knee surgery in 2012, but refused to do anything about it other than buy bigger clothes. It took my boyfriend taking a picture of

me to see just how big I had gotten. I was disgusted and embarrassed by what I saw. I couldn't believe I had gone from 135 [pounds] to 190 [pounds]. For me it wasn't about the food I was eating but about how often I would eat. If I missed breakfast and lunch, I would binge eat at dinner then go to bed if I ate at all (working in base deployments we were always busy).

One day, after learning I could be discharged from the Air Force for failing to meet fitness standards, I decided to go to the gym. While I was there I heard this lady teaching a spin class. I couldn't believe how she was yelling at these ladies and they were actually enjoying it. I poked my head in but quickly decided this was not for me. This lady left her class and followed me. I will never forget the words she spoke to me; she said "if you truly want to change how you look on the outside, it has to start with how you see yourself on the inside." I just looked at her with the deer caught in the headlights look and then she said "if you are serious about losing weight then meet me back here at 4:30 am tomorrow morning. If not, then I will see you around the gym". I was actually shocked because I had never met anyone who actually was willing to help me lose weight. I took a chance and showed up at 4:30 the next morning and all I can say is, this lady was so dedicated to helping others better themselves through nutrition and fitness that I immediately decided I wanted to change my lifestyle for the better. She took her time with me and helped me build the confidence I needed to start loving myself.

In three months, I went from 185 pounds, size 18, to 170 pounds, size 16, scoring 85% on my fitness test. This was a big deal to me. I thank God every day that he put that special lady in my life. When I retired in 2017, I was down to 160 pounds, size 12, and toned. I never felt better in my life. Until this day I still use my food journal as well as a fitness journal and often looked back over my progress over the years. I made a promise to myself that I would never let myself get that big ever again.

Jamie's story was so impactful to me. I wish I could meet the lady who changed her life because that is my mission as well. This is also why I feel, as personal trainers and service providers, we need to work together to inspire and empower as many people as possible. While I mostly focus on women, men need to learn these tools as well. It is up to us to change the game. It starts with how you treat people. That woman changed Jamie's life forever. Think about this when you see someone struggling in the gym. You may give that person hope by offering to help them, instead of judging them.

> This verse from Ecclesiastes says it the best: *"The end of a matter is better than its beginning, and patience is better than pride."*
> – Ecclesiastes 7:8

I am guilty of allowing pride to keep me from accomplishing great things in my life. It also kept me from allowing myself to love and grow as a person and a mom. Once I let my pride down and started realizing I was NOT in control of everything, so many things began to change for me. Doors began to open and I became truly enlightened.

I truly pray that you will continue the journey you have started through your reading and the assignments in this book. I pray that you have learned tools that will allow you to stop letting fear run you. I pray that you never give up on yourself and that you continue to work through the challenges you will face each day.

I would be lying to you if I said any of this was going to be easy. Fact is, implementing new habits into our lives is one of the most difficult things we will encounter. It is very easy for us to point out what is wrong with others, but turning the mirror around on ourselves is humbling. For those of us who are prideful, we can tend to allow that pride to keep us from gaining knowledge and growing in our purpose. I know this first-hand. It took me losing almost everything and for life to basically just stop, for me to finally stop trying to keep up with those who were money-driven. I am not like them. I am driven by the ability to help others become healthier and happier. This leads them to fulfillment and it motivates me to learn even more so that I can continue to share and help others grow. While I do need income in order to keep and run the business, it's not my main driver. It's not why I started this. It has become a reward for the gift I have been provided with.

My promise to you is this: if you read this book with an open mind and implemented the tools you were given (including the worksheets provided), you will be able to make lasting change in many areas of your life. You must be willing to let go of any pride you are still holding onto and learn to be patient.

What you have learned in this book is not a temporary fix. It is not me telling you exactly how to live your life. These are tools that were provided to me over years of mistakes and experience. These are lessons and tools you too can use and implement for the rest of your life. First, I highly urge you to open yourself up to the possibilities. If you have not submitted yourself to our Lord, this may be the first step in your life that should be taken. I say this because before I submitted myself, I was a lost cause. If you have already done this, you can probably relate. When we submit ourselves and let go of our pride, we are able to truly learn more than we ever imagined.

The Lord has granted me the ability to write this book. It is something I never thought possible, yet here it is. In whatever you choose, just remember – in order for any of it to have a lasting effect in a positive way, you have to make it a lifestyle. If you give up on yourself and discontinue what you started, you will resort back to your old life. It is more comfortable there, but I challenge you to use the tools here and actually learn more about yourself. You can do all things through Christ who strengthens you. We all can! Know that you are fearfully and wonderfully made. Know that you are important to your families, your co-workers, and your acquaintances. You have the ability to set the precedence for what happens in your life. I leave it up to you now to do just that.

If all else fails, *"Trust in the Lord with all your heart and lean not on your own understanding"* Proverbs 3:5.

When you feel like you just want to give up (and believe me when I say I have been there many times), I urge you to remember why you began. Why did you want to learn more? Remember that God put us in charge of protecting these temples – our bodies. He also gave His son to forgive us for our sins. We must forgive ourselves of any wrongdoing and proceed with the path He always had in front of us. All we have to do is ... Go.

Conclusion

In this book, you learned about mindset development, time management, self-care, nutrition, exercise, and making it a lifestyle. I have given you a snippet of how I used these tools to help me in my life and how others are succeeding by using them as well. Please know that I do not make anything up. I have put a ton of time and effort into learning these concepts. When people see me now and think I have it all together, I appreciate that because they didn't see the times I was completely lost and felt there was no end to the chaos. They didn't see me at my lowest points in life. They weren't there when I wanted it all to end so badly to the point where I thought about doing it myself.

This book comes from complete transparency and genuineness. I am one of your biggest fans (you should be your ultimate fan). I want you to stop holding yourself back. I want you to free yourself from your own personal bondage. I want you to know that you don't have to conform or be like others. It's ok to be you. I want all this for you. However, you have to want it for yourself.

Throughout this book, I have shared some stories that I pray will allow you to see that we all have a journey. Every day, I must be aware of my responses to things and realize that I could easily go right back to where I was, spiritually and physically. What I have done is chosen to no longer live like I did before. I choose to listen to my calling. I choose to live a life filled with serving others. I choose to be happy and grateful for what I have instead of allowing lack to take over. I choose these things in Jesus' name because He paid the ultimate sacrifice so that we could make these choices and repent for any wrong-doing. He sacrificed so we could be whole again. It doesn't matter how much you have been broken down in your life. What matters now is that you allow yourself to progress and enjoy the journey, just as I and so many others have.

Maybe you need to take some time away from everyone and everything in order to truly reflect. Maybe you are so proud that you are not willing to take a good look at yourself. However, I will tell you from experience that being willing to turn the mirror around and examine yourself is the single most freeing thing you can do. Is it easy? Not at all. If it were easy, we would all be more willing to do it earlier in our lives. We go through life thinking we are good to go. However, we often don't realize that we sabotage ourselves daily.

It's time to allow yourself to become happy and be fulfilled. It's time you put into practice the tools you have learned here. It's time you stop worrying about what others will think or how many "friends" you may lose and focus on self-satisfaction. It's time to live. Otherwise, all we do is end up with regrets. I don't know about you, but I no longer need regrets in my life. Life is too short. We are here for a short period of time to make a mark on this earth. We are put here to serve others and take care of our temples. We are extraordinary. In knowing that, mediocre and comfort should no longer be an option. Get out. Challenge yourself. Conquer your fears. There are no limits except those we set upon ourselves. Just ... GO!

Resources

[1]Barban, J. (2016). *The Venus Factor. 12-Week Fat Loss System.* StreengthWorks International Publishing, Inc.

[2]Celerier, E. (2020). Release Forgiveness Towards Others and Yourself. Retrieved Jan 5, 2020 from https://www.bible.com/en/reading-plans/10998.

[3]Child Welfare Information Gateway. (2016). *Impact on Children and Youth.* Retrieved December 8, 2019 from https://www.childwelfare.gov/topics/systemwide/domviolence/impact/children-youth/

[4]Duhigg, C. (2012). *The Power of Habit: Why We Do What We Do in Life and Business.* Random House Trade Paperbacks: New York.

[5]Gornia, C. (2019). 22 Ways to Wake Up and Feel Super Positive for the Day. Lifehack.org. Retrieved May 13, 2019 from https://www.lifehack.org/articles/lifestyle/22-ways-wake-and-feel-super-positive-for-the-day.html.

[6]Hill, N. (2005). *Think and Grow Rich, Revision.* Revised and Expanded for the 21st Century by Dr. Arthur R. Pell. JMW Group, Inc: New York.

[7]Kennedy, T. (2020). The Ultimate Morning Routine to Make You Happy and Productive All Day. Retrieved December 12, 2019 from https://www.lifehack.org/768258/morning-routine-to-make-your-day

[8]McGee, R. (2003). *The Search for Significance.* Nashville, TN: Thomas -Nelson, Inc.

[9] Robbins, T. (2020). What's Your Morning Ritual? Retrieved January 16, 2020 from https://www.tonyrobbins.com/mind-meaning/whats-your-morning-ritual/

[10] National Academy of Sports Medicine. (2018). Fitness Nutrition Specialist Certification.

[11] The Four Step Plan on How to Create Your Own Affirmations. (2019). Retrieved from http://www.thelawofattraction.com/how-create-own-affirmations/

[12] Top 10 Benefits of Regular Physical Activity. (2019). Retrieved May 8, 2019 from http://www.secondscount.org/heart-resources/heart-resources-detail?cid=f32db674-f604-4483-a6fd-31081cf66065&gclid=Cj0KCQjwn8_mBRCLARIsAKxi0GLsmT-F9aM4OWo1DUUfY9p_SCqF8GWJRSUTfpqTrR6iDfxE6ieKF5QaAjZiEALw_wcB#.XNPX-RNicWo.

[13] USGS.gov. (2019). The Water in You: Water and the Human Body. Retrieved December 25, 2019 from https://www.usgs.gov/special-topic/water-science-school/science/water-you-water-and-human-body?qt-science_center_objects=0#qt-science_center_objects

[14] Vocabulary.com. (2020). Proactive/Reactive Definitions. Retrieved December 10, 2019 from www.vocabulary.com.

[15] YMCA. (2020). Five Benefits of Strength Training for Women. Retrieved January 17, 2020 from https://lafayettefamilyymca.org/five-benefits-of-strength-training-for-women/

Appendix – Worksheets for Continuation

Congratulations on taking the first steps towards a life of fulfillment and happiness. In order to be happy, you must be fulfilled. As you progress through these worksheets, I urge you to get an accountability partner. As my gift to you, I will be that for you for 30 days. All you have to do is email me at jodiwatkins@2bepicfn.com. Each worksheet contains helpful tips and questions that really will get you thinking more. Accompanying these worksheets with each chapter can truly be an amazing experience for you and I pray you will continue using the tools you have learned throughout this book and in the worksheets. You are enough. You are blessed beyond belief and you are blessing me by allowing me to be a part of your journey. Thank you and God bless!

1.1 Worksheet 1 - Mindset/Feelings/Stress Management Worksheet

In order to get our own mental limitations, we must first address them. We will focus on mindset development here and our feelings. We will also address stress management and how to conquer feelings of being overwhelmed and overtasked. This worksheet will allow you to pinpoint the event(s) that trigger stress or feelings of being overwhelmed. We will focus on things that might be distracting you from your true purpose and potential. As humans, we are natural reactors (see my blog at www.2bepicfn.com about being proactive versus reactive). We react to situations instead of acting on what we do have control over – ourselves. In order to begin learning how to undo this reactionary phase, it is important to notice when we are getting stressed or overwhelmed so we can control how we react. It may be as simple as taking a deep breath and thinking about all the good in our lives, instead of focusing on that one bad thing. If we focus on the negative, we are going to continue going into a negative space. However, if we focus on the positives in our lives, we are more often going to be able to overcome adverse situations that would normally set us over the edge. For some of us, thinking more positively is not all that difficult. For some, it is easier not to share our emotions. Many people go through trauma in their early lives that dictate how they respond later in life. In order to truly be successful this week, it will be vital to address situations that may be subconsciously holding you back and allow yourself to let them go. In order to bring in the new, we must let go of the old. I had to do a LOT of work in this area, but I will attest that it has been a truly freeing experience. This is not something you will most likely perfect; however, as long as you are able to stop yourself from reacting beforehand, you are going to notice that you are far more satisfied with what is going on in your life and you have a better way of dealing with things that are out of your control. Remember that you can only control you. Once you have learned the tactics needed to focus on you, you will see that your reactions become positive actions and enable you to be more productive over a long period of time. We are going to address some of the feelings and fears that may be holding you back and we are going to get you working on becoming more aware so that you can truly excel in the future with anything you are called to do. I am so happy you are making this amazing commitment to yourself! I look forward to working with you to ensure you are successful in your journey!

Be Free Through Forgiveness of Others and YOURSELF!

> *"Be kind and compassionate to one another, forgiving each other, just as in Christ God forgave you."*
> — Ephesians 4:32

The Feeling Wheel:

> "The Feeling Wheel is a visual tool designed to help people recognize and identify their own feelings. When a person is asked to express feelings, there is frequently a real vagueness in identifying the way he or she feels ...

[we say] I feel good, I feel bad, I feel better, I feel worse, I'm okay."[8] We aren't normally comfortable with telling how we truly feel. Think about your daily interactions. How often do you really tell people how you feel? This is something I really had to work on because until I started opening up more, my relationships were not near as deep as they are now. They were superficial, because I was being superficial. The next time you have a conversation with someone, try opening up just a little more. Not too much, but just enough to where you feel as though you addressed any concerns you may have had. This is even more important in the work I do now. If I am not comfortable with sharing myself with others, how can I expect them to share themselves with me on a more intimate level? As we continue this program, I urge you to be open in your feelings and thoughts. It may feel different at first and be challenging, but you may just find that your experience is so much better just because you made the choice to be all in on a more emotional level. Let's begin this week's questionnaire with these thoughts in mind.

1. Has there ever been any trauma in your life that made you feel less than adequate?

Your answer:

1. Have you ever felt you weren't truly worthy of all good things in your life? If so, how did this impact your daily decisions? If you are still going through it, would you be willing to start writing down daily affirmations to help you confirm your self-worth?

Your answer:

2. Briefly describe a stressful situation you are currently going through.

Your answer:

3. What are the signals or physical symptoms you incur as a result of this stress?

Your answer:

4. Do you think your expectations for yourself and comparisons to others impact your daily stress? For example, if you meet someone your age who has accomplished more or you think about where you used to be compared to where you are now, does this impact you in a negative way?

Your answer:

5. Do you get down on yourself if you don't accomplish something you set out to do? ★

Your answer:

6. If you answered "yes" to the above question, what are some things you currently do in order to get into a better place? If you do not currently have a routine here, please let me know and we can talk about some ideas that may help you through this area.

Your answer:

7. What aspects of your stress do you feel you are unable to control?

Your answer:

8. Write down some things that you should say to yourself when you start feeling less than adequate?

Your answer:

9. When you are confronted with a stressful situation, do you get angry and overwhelmed or are you able to control yourself by stepping back, taking a deep breath, thinking about all the positives in your life, and THEN tackling the issue at hand more strategically and less emotionally?

Your answer:

10. How many tasks do you feel you must achieve on a daily basis? Do these tasks make you feel overwhelmed?

Your answer:

11. Research shows it can take up to 10 weeks to form a new habit. If your old habits involve stress and feelings of being overwhelmed, I challenge you to take a few minutes to write down your daily feelings in a journal or calendar describing the situations and your actions towards them. Find an accountability partner (or allow me to be that for you) and discuss your answer with that person. Allow him or her to think about this as well and help one another through the internal battle as you continue your journey.

12. Do you understand that learning how to manage your feelings and stress level will allow you to be successful in other areas of your life and also allow you to be more fulfilled at the end of the day?

Your answer:

Summary

Thank you for filling out the worksheet. You may notice that things begin to come together once you learn how to manage your feelings and the stress in your life. Learning how to love yourself is important because we often become reactive due to lack of self-confidence or lowered feelings of self-worth. While it is not an easy task to break old habits, it is important to achieving a life of total health, wellness, and fulfillment in this program. Thank you again for being part of this movement! I appreciate you and your willingness to allow me to guide you through and fulfill your goals.

1.2 Worksheet 2 – Time Management

Welcome to the Assignment and Tools Worksheet. We are now focusing on Time Management. It is important to realize what we spend our time on mostly so that we can begin to see a better work/life balance in the future. We have so many things that demand our time. It is important to examine each area of where we spend our most valuable asset - time. If we are spending more time in an area that is making another area more overwhelming, it is important to become aware of this so we can make a plan to do better. It is so easy to waste time. It is easy to let time slip away. It is also easy to spend more time in one area of our lives to where it affects other areas. Therefore, this worksheet will help you become more aware of where you spend your time so that you can truly evaluate if these areas are positively or negatively impacting your life and those around you.

It's "Time" to do an Audit on Your Most Valuable Asset

There are so many resources out there that tell us how to make better use of our time, but what we often fail to do is use our number one resource - God. How often do we just lunge into tasks without consulting the one who made us? He is our ultimate resource and He will guide us if we allow Him to. In the meantime, as we partner with Him, we must also become aware of ourselves. This is our reality check. This is where we look at all the areas of our lives and ask ourselves this question: Where do we spend most of our time? Is that time benefitting us or not? Is it best to just shut down when we have a lot on our plate or just tackle things a little at a time so they don't become so overwhelming in the end? Let's look further into how we can better manage our time.

1. Have you ever done a true audit on your time? This is just like doing a financial audit. We look at where we are spending most of our time and we write down these areas giving room to rank them in priority.

Your answer:

2. Use a larger notebook (if you ordered the accompanying kit from https://www.2bepicfn.com/store/total-health-life-gift-box, you were provided a notebook to use and some examples of how to proceed with your scheduling). Write down all the areas of your life that you spend time on. Leave room underneath each subject to write a number under it ranking it in priority. Some examples of subjects could be: God, Family, School, Self-Care, etc. Once you have done this, please write down if you feel this was helpful and how it impacted your day. Was THIS a good use of your time? (P.S. If you haven't ever added Self-Care into your life, it's time to start now)

Your answer:

3. Have you been practicing only writing down THREE extra MAIN tasks each day that you must accomplish? We may have other little things, but we should never add more than three large tasks in a day. When it comes to what I call "sitting" tasks you do on a daily basis, would you consider setting a timer so that you not only keep your mind from wandering, but you also stay fresh and keep yourself from straying into an area that was not on your list? I suggest the 30-minute timer. 30 minutes for the task, then 10 minutes to decompress, walk

around, do something in the house that won't take too long, whatever the case may be. Then go back to what you were doing and continue to set the timer. Just make sure you don't take more than a 10-minute break. Otherwise, you may end up not completing the main task you set out to finish.

Your answer:

4. A tip for homework assignments for those in further education: Block off a certain amount of time to complete assignments, setting timers for mental breaks. Pray before you begin that God will give you the strength to get through the assignment and allow you to see clearly. You have everything in you to succeed. You just have to fight the urge of getting frustrated and know that may just mean you need to take a little break and come back. Do you feel this would be helpful for those assignments that seem stressful?

Your answer:

5. Plan ahead: In this stage of the program, I would like you to practice planning ahead. Build a schedule for the following day the day before. You should already know at least a day ahead what you have on your plate for the following day. Build a schedule and do what you can when you can. That way, when life happens, you won't be so overwhelmed and you will have accomplished the important tasks for the day. Planning ahead is vital in most areas of our lives. While we can't predict

everything, if we are ready for anything, we are already a step ahead of whatever else we may encounter. Have you ever done this before? If so, did you stick to it? Why or why not? Remember that consistency is key.

Your answer:

6. Tip: Spend your mornings on your most important tasks. What are your most important tasks that stay consistent each day? For me, it is God, Family, then making sure I have what I need for the day. I don't get on my phone until the most important tasks that have to be done first thing in the morning are completed. Then I may take a break, but I then begin to do what else I had to get done. I do the tasks that are required of me for that day before I allow myself to get distracted by the rest of the world. What do you do in your mornings? Do you give yourself some "me time" (this could be spiritual and/or physical-exercise) before you have to rush into your other obligations? If not, would you be willing to begin doing this? See how this might positively affect your day.

Your answer:

7. Tip: Learn to delegate. Currently, in our house, it is my almost 10-year-old and myself. However, when there are things she can help with, I ask for her help. Do you get your family involved with helping you around the house or do you try to do everything yourself? This is an important thing to do in business as well, no matter what you do.

While you may not know it, I know that I cannot change you or make you do anything you do not want to do. I give you the tools and then I "delegate" you to put the tools to use. If you are the only person in your business (or the one you intend to build), you will want to have a way to make sure it isn't all on your shoulders. By trying to do it all, you are not only depriving those around you of the knowledge you hold, but you are also setting yourself up to become more overwhelmed. Talk about your goals with those around you. You never know who might be willing to help you get even further than you can go alone. We are not meant to work alone. We can always use a wingman!

Your answer:

8. Tip: Get organized. I am completely at fault for this. Things pile up and then I have often not known where to start. My advice is doing something I still have to force myself to do - get organized. We tend to spend more time looking for stuff we lost than we need to. Then we spend money replacing what we lost. It's best to just stay organized so we can always find things when we need them. How organized are you when it comes to being able to find things when you need them?

Your answer:

9. Tip: Use an online calendar. This is the one I absolutely HATED! I would carry a paper calendar around with me. The only problem was, what if I forgot that calendar? Also, I began to use an online

call scheduling system that did NOT tie into my paper calendar. So I would end up being booked for something when I had something else going on. While I still use a paper calendar for backup, I do not rely on it anymore. Do you currently use an online calendar? Do you put appointments in that calendar as soon as they are booked? Why or why not?

Your answer:

10. Always remember, it's progress over perfection. If you are spending all your time trying to be perfect, you might want to re-evaluate your thought process. Perfect doesn't exist. Now, can we strive to be better? OF COURSE! But don't spend your time trying to achieve something that isn't actually attainable. Is it good to put effort into what you do so that you have a better outcome? OF COURSE! Just know that it doesn't mean you should spend hours upon hours trying to make something be what it can't be. We are human and we will make mistakes. Do you feel as though you are a perfectionist? If so, you may not know it, but you will spend so much time on a task trying to perfect it that you will risk not getting other things done that day. So how productive are you really being at that point?

Your answer:

11. Ever heard the saying, "Just Say No!" Sometimes, we have to say no. We are only one person, so we can't achieve EVERYTHING, even if

we want to. If we always keep in mind, God, Family, Self-Care, then Work, we will learn to keep our priorities where they belong and not go too far in any other direction. Do you often find yourself saying "Yes" to the point where you begin to realize you overtasked yourself? When someone asks you to do something, tell them you will get back to them before agreeing right there on the spot. Then check your calendar and make sure you can accommodate them without putting more stress on yourself.

Your answer:

12. Instill habits that will benefit you in the long run. I know we have covered a lot this week. Do you feel as though some of these things will help you gain more time in your day? I'd love to hear any wins you have or any ways you are going to begin using this information.

Your answer:

Summary

Thank you for filling out the worksheet. You may notice that things begin to come together once you learn how to audit your time or manage it. You may find areas in which you can gain some time back if you become more aware of where you are spending it. While it is not an easy task to break old habits, it is important to achieving a life of total health, wellness, and fulfillment in this program. Thank you again for being part of this movement! I appreciate you and your willingness to allow me to guide you through and fulfill your goals.

1.3 Worksheet 3 - Self Care Worksheet

Welcome to this section's Assignment and Tools Worksheet. We now are focusing on Self Care. We must always remember that if we are not willing to take care of ourselves, it will almost impossible to truly show up for others. Wake up grateful and remember that each day is not promised. Each day is a blessing and we have to remember that in order to truly enjoy the blessings we are given, we have to make time for ourselves to decompress and just BE ... this is so hard for most of us, especially those of us who are moms ... but it is so important. As we continue this journey, allow yourself to take some time for yourself. You may just find that it allows you to be more productive during the day and get through the times when "life happens" a whole lot better. Mindset is everything. Don't allow yourself to get overwhelmed. You have the power to commit to you. Why not begin today if this is something you struggle with currently. All it takes is starting and being patient. Nothing happens overnight!

> *"He helps tired people be strong. He gives power to those without it."*
>
> – Isaiah 40:29

I Give You Permission to Take Care of YOU! Let the Lord Guide You.

There are so many resources out there that tell us how to take better care of ourselves, but what we fail to remember is that God wants us to take care of ourselves. He wants us to know we have a purpose and that if we treat ourselves correctly, we will truly be able to fulfill the gifts in which HE has given us. How often do we just lunge into tasks without consulting the one who made us? He is our ultimate resource and He will guide us if we allow Him to. In the meantime, as we partner with Him, we must also become aware of ourselves. This is our reality check. This is where we look at all the areas of our lives and ask ourselves another question: Do we take care of ourselves before we try to tackle life?

1. What is the first thing you say to yourself in the morning?

Your answer:

2. In a small notebook (the accompanying kit has a notebook for this portion), I urge you to begin writing positive things about yourself each day to help you stay in a positive mindset and not get down on yourself when you are less than perfect? Is this something you are willing to do? Why or why not?

Your answer:

3. Do you wake up grateful for what you have or do you immediately think about what you need to do for the day?

Your answer:

4. What is something you can do for yourself that you have been neglecting?

Your answer:

5. Don't forget the tips in Chapter 3 that help you crush your morning:

- Consider what makes you happy
- Give gratitude
- Relax your body
- Focus on breathing
- Don't attach to your negative thoughts
- Stay off social media
- Prepare a delicious breakfast
- Establish a meditation practice
- Don't check your phone until much later.
- Do something physical (go for a run or do some sort of cardio, yoga, or something that will allow you to feel more energized first thing)
- Create a routine that includes morning self-care
- Wake up to a clean room (tidy up the night before so you don't wake up with chores to do)
- Ask yourself, "How can I make today amazing?"
- Smile regardless of how you might feel at first.

How can you use these tips to stay on track and stay positive each day?

Your answer:

6. How did Chapter 3 help you think more about how you do things currently? What are some things you have learned so far and what are some wins you have encountered?

Your answer:

7. Get organized. I am completely at fault of this. Things pile up and then I have often not known where to start. My advice is doing something I still have to force myself to do – get organized. We tend to spend more time looking for stuff we lost than we need to. Then we spend money replacing what we lost. It's best to just stay organized so we can always find things when we need them. How organized are you when it comes to being able to find things when you need them?

Your answer:

8. Always remember, it's progress over perfection. You are not going to be 100% with everything. How has this affected your daily tasks?

Your answer:

9. Do you have any questions about what we have gone over in this worksheet? If so, please state them below. You may also use this space to elaborate on some things you are currently doing to help you take care of yourself and get into a positive state of mind.

Your answer:

Summary

Thank you for filling out the worksheet. You may notice that things begin to come together once you learn how to audit your time or manage it. You may find areas in which you can gain some time back if you become more aware of where you are spending it. While it is not an easy task to break old habits, it is important to achieving a life of total health, wellness, and fulfillment in this program. Thank you again for being part of this movement! I appreciate you and your willingness to allow me to guide you through and fulfill your goals.

1.4 Worksheet 4 - Nutrition Worksheet

Welcome to this Assignment and Tools Worksheet. In the accompanying chapter, we focused on Nutrition. Wouldn't it be nice if God would write a "Healthy Living Plan" for us to follow? It would completely take all the guesswork out of it! Well, over the course of the last 6 years and some change, I have learned what we all need to know … there is

NO one formula in this area. It is a lot of trial and error and learning what works for YOU. No one wants to hear that, but it is the truth. This is the area we ALL struggled with at some point and may still struggle with. There are so many "gurus" out there telling us what we should eat, when we should eat it, how we should eat it. They tell us to take out food groups and macronutrient groups, leaving us even more confused and lethargic because we aren't getting what our body's need. Through tons of research and education, I can finally say I do NOT have to diet in order to maintain a healthy lifestyle. I would be doing you an injustice if I were to keep all this information to myself. So here's my challenge to you: take the information and USE it. I can guarantee that if you are willing to put more of your effort into this portion of your program and BALANCE it with the rest of your life, you can and will achieve any goal or body look you yearn for. Now, with that said, God also wants us to love ourselves for WHO WE ARE. We should NEVER be in competition with anyone else. We can use others as inspiration, but it's best to remember why you are doing what you are doing. What motivates you? Being healthy enough to work hard and provide for your family? To keep up with your kids (I know this one is definitely what keeps me going)? Take fun vacations? Enjoy hobbies you love? Volunteer in the community? Serve your church? The healthier you are, the more likely you will get to enjoy all the above and more! Care for your temple. This means you must FUEL your body properly. What happens if you go to the gas station to put gas in your car and you don't put enough? It runs out of gas faster. If you don't put the proper fuel in it? It sputters and doesn't have the correct functioning properties, aka energy. What if you put too much fuel in your car? It overflows! This is where we go back to the basis of this entire program: BALANCE. In everything we do, including nutrition, we must find the proper balance for ourselves. We have a tracker in our car right? A gauge that tells us how much fuel we have versus what we need and when we are running low. Our bodies have a gauge as well. The problem is, we often don't listen. When we run low on energy, most of us don't think about proper nutrition as being the factor that could help in that area. What if we often get sick? Could it be that we aren't getting enough fruits and vegetables? This is where Juice Plus comes into play (natural resource in a capsule for a quick resolution to getting the amount of MICROnutrients we need). This is especially important for children and even more important for picky children. Check out my Juice Plus website at http://jodiwatkins.juiceplus.com or the tower garden (if you like to grow your own fruits and veggies) at http://jodiwatkins.towergarden.com. Having issues getting the proper amount of protein your body needs or maybe you would like to look at possible options for a meal on the go? Check out http://1stphorm.com/jodionamission for the most quality supplements on the market and use my link for free shipping! I am your coach and I am here to answer any questions you may have on any products. Here to help in any way I can. So, let's get started on how to conquer this portion of your life.

It's Time to Learn How to Fuel Your Body Properly!

Why is it so difficult to learn how to eat? For one, there are a million "gurus" out there who are experts in how you should eat. They give you a meal plan or "diet." They tell you that you have to restrict whole food groups in order to reach your goals. However, when it comes down to it, doing something differently, no matter what it is, has to be your choice. You have to feel "led" to it by your own free will. So what it different about what I teach? First, it is based off science and research. Also, it is sustainable for life and allows you to fuel your body as it needs to be fueled, with the proper amount of fuel and ingredients. Proverbs 3:13 says, *"blessed are those who find wisdom, who gain understanding."* Verses 19-20 say, *"By wisdom the Lord laid the earth's foundations, by understanding He set the heavens in place; by His knowledge the watery depths were divided, and the clouds let drop the dew."* The Lord has allowed me to accumulate more wisdom in the area of nutrition to empower you to make choices based off facts rather than someone's opinion. I can always share what has helped me, but I must also provide you with facts of why it helped and why it became my go to for how I live. I provide the tools, you implement them with patience and diligence, and one day, you will be able to share this with someone else you know and love. It's the only process that has yet to falter. No fad diet can ever beat proven science. It just won't happen. Let's get started, shall we?

1. Now that we have talked about schedules and setting time slots for things you have to get done, it's time to use the same principles to

conquer this area of your program. Have you ever thought about what you were going to eat before you ate it? How difficult would it be to plan your meals out beforehand?

Your answer

2. If you are using the My Fitness Pal app, you can easily log in your main meals for the day. This will limit the amount of time you spend tracking your foods as you go. Is this something you are willing to try in order to help you establish a better eating routine?

Your answer

3. Challenge: Log your main meals in either the day before or sometime in the morning before your day gets busy for the next week. Come back to this area and answer the following question: was it as difficult as you thought it would be in your head?

Yes
No

4. Now that you have your main meals logged, you can keep a notebook on you (if that is easier for you), and write in any extra food you take in throughout the day. Just remember, if you use a notebook, you don't want to wait until the end of the day to log your foods into the app. Preferably, you want to add food in before you eat them. Otherwise, you may find at the end of the day that you were way off in calorie intake, macronutrient intake, and/or micronutrient intake (fiber, sugar, iron, etc). Do you understand why it's actually better to log your food before you eat them?

Yes
No

5. Remember: This is NOT a diet or a "get-skinny quick" option. This is an option that will allow you to really LEARN your body's needs so that you can continue to fuel it properly depending on changes in the environment, physical activity, physical attributes, etc. Are you willing to incorporate this for the duration of your program in order to ensure you have learned what your body needs?

Yes
No

6. This is the part of the program where people normally check out. Don't you keep track of your finances? Why not keep track of what you put in your body. To me, that is far more important in living a healthier lifestyle. I urge you to follow the guidelines we have already instilled when it comes to schedules and pre-planning in this area as well. Planning ahead in this area is just as important for optimal health and will keep you from having to do a memory jog at the end of the day. Side note, adding my foods into the food journal beforehand also allows me to easily prep my foods the next day if I have a long day ahead, such as when I was doing personal training regularly or worked all day. Do you understand that planning ahead in this area allows you to stay balanced and not get overwhelmed? What are your thoughts on this?

Your answer

7. I always say progress over perfection because if you strive for perfection, you will let yourself down 100% of the time. Strive to do your best in all areas of your life. Allow this portion of your program to be a guide that will help you into the future. Do not fear the unknown. Be secure knowing that you are doing something most people aren't willing to do. How does that make you feel?

Your answer

8. I'd love to hear your feedback from Chapter 4. Please let me know what you liked/didn't like and if you would like to maybe see anything else added into the chapter. You can email me directly at jodiwatkins@2bepicfn.com. Thank you!

Summary

Nutrition and learning how to eat, what to eat, and how much to eat is crucial when it comes to achieving our body's full potential. Maybe you don't have a specific goal in mind. Nevertheless, you will find that by taking the principles you are already applying in other areas and applying it here, you will learn more and more about yourself and be able to share it with others. I appreciate your continuous feedback in helping me solidify this program. Have a great week!

1.5 Worksheet 5 - Exercise Worksheet

Welcome to the Assignment and Tools Worksheet for Chapter 5. This week, we focused on Exercise and why it is important to balance cardio with strength training. You want to make sure if you hire someone to help you with your exercise goals, they have experience and can properly guide you. You also want to ensure they are a great fit for YOU. Interview them, ask them questions, find out if they truly have what it takes to guide you. When you are in the gym, make sure you know how to work the machines and do any exercises properly. Don't just ask anyone. Ask a trained professional. Strength training is beneficial for everyone. For women, it helps with hormonal balance and combating osteoporosis. It limits deterioration in joints and allows you to be stronger for longer!

> *"If any of you lack wisdom, you should ask God, who gives generously to all without finding fault, and it will be given to you."*
> – James 1:5

Knowing How to Balance Cardio with Strength Training is Important - 5 Benefits of Strength Training for Women:

1 Corinthians 3:17 says, *"If anyone destroys God's temple, God will destroy that person; for God's temple is sacred, and you together are that temple."* If God charges us to take care of His temple, why is it so difficult for us to do want to find answers so that we can truly do everything in our power to take care of these temples we have been given? I, too, took my temple for granted for many years. However, through a major occurrence in my life, I realized just how important it was to take care of this temple in all ways possible. I will never say I have total control. I have no idea where my life will take me or how long I have left on this earth. However, I CAN make it a point to do everything in my power to seek information that will help me take care of myself and combat things that ARE in my control. Most women are quick to begin a cardiovascular exercise program, and that is awesome, especially for those who are just starting out. Anything is better than nothing all day long.

However, learning how to lift weights has benefits for women that most are not aware of. Want to lose body fat quickly? Implementing regular strength training into your routine is one of the quickest ways to lose body fat (along with proper fuel intake of course). Women, on average, store at least 10% more body fat than men. That means it's more difficult for us to lose body fat. However, it isn't impossible. Implement a balance of cardio and strength training and see what happens. You may be surprised. MYTH BUSTER: You are NOT going to get "bulky" if you lift weights.

Did you know that most of the muscular women you see have that muscle because they worked REALLY hard to get it? Maybe it was through nutrition (eating a lot more than we burn to develop the muscle and eating a lot of protein, which is not what most of the women in the world do ... so just lifting weights doesn't give you more muscle than you want. There are other things involved in that portion of it all).

INCREASES YOUR RMR

What lifting weights WILL do is allow you to feel more confident and be stronger. Burn more calories ALL DAY LONG with strength training. One study found that "regular strength training can increase your RMR - Resting Metabolic Rate - by about 5%. This means your body burns more calories throughout the day - even while you're NOT working out. The higher your RMR, the faster you burn fat, and the quicker you lose weight." (Study information found on the Lafayette Family YMCA Website — see resource list for YMCA). Strength training in women decreases the likelihood of developing osteoporosis. Strength training has been proven to increase bone density, which in turn, decreases the development of osteoporosis (loss of bone density).

REDUCES RISK OF HEART DISEASE

One other thing strength training does is help reduce the risk of heart disease. If you have any form of heart disease in your family, I highly recommend adding a good strength training program into your routine. Cardiovascular exercise is great, and strength training doesn't have to be done everyday, but a balance of both along with proper nutrition is the best way to reach your overall health and wellness goals!

While strength training surely has its benefits for women, men benefit highly as well the more they age. A man who learns and implements knowledge in strength training allows his body to be stronger and healthier. His metabolism gets a boost as well. Furthermore, strengthening the muscles allows the tendons, ligaments, bones, and joints, to become stronger also. For men, strength training is also the best way to burn calories and gain lean muscle mass while ditching the body fat. Men naturally can have less body fat than women, so with the proper nutrient balance, a man can also transform his body through a proper exercise program and instruction on lifting safely and effectively.

1. Before going through this program, were you aware of the benefits of strength training when it came to exercise in general?

Your answer

2. After reading the benefits of strength training, do you feel this is something you will want to implement?

Yes
No

3. Do you understand that exercise in general is very beneficial and that adding strength training is just another way to challenge yourself and feel better about your total health plan?

Yes
No

4. What do you think you may start doing differently now that you are armed with more wisdom?

Your answer

5. If you already exercise regularly, I challenge you to begin implementing (2) days of strength training into your week, then work up to (3) days. Do you think this is a reasonable promise you can make to yourself?

Yes
No

6. Have you ever worked with a professional when implementing a fitness program? Why or why not?

Your answer

7. Do you understand how important it is to seek out proper information and guidance when you are first starting out so that you can learn correctly how to maintain a lifestyle of different exercise styles?

Yes
No

What was your biggest takeaway from this portion of the book? Please email your answers to jodiwatkins@2bepicfn.com.

Your answer

Summary

Exercise definitely has its benefits when it comes to programming a routine for yourself. I hope that you have learned a lot about why strength training is so important for women. I also hope you know you don't need a gym membership. Strength training comes in all forms. Your body makes an amazing weight if used properly. I hope you have learned a lot from this book and you will want to learn more. If you are interested in customized programming, please go to https://www.trainerize.me/profile/2bepicfn to see what is available to you. I am grateful to have the opportunity to pour this information out to you and continue to work toward my mission of encouraging healthier lifestyles all over the world!

1.6 Worksheet 6 - Consistency: Practice Makes Better

"The end of a matter is better than its beginning, and patience is better than pride."

– Ecclesiastes 7:8.

Thank you so much for purchasing this book and reading it to the end. I hope you had a bit of a breakthrough so you can begin to tackle those areas which have been holding you back.

Week 6 is all about consistency and progression. It's about learning how to continue using the tools you have received and holding yourself accountable in all areas of your life. Thank you so much for your time. I have truly enjoyed this experience and am grateful for the opportunity to have served you. I am beyond grateful to God for allowing me the opportunity and giving me the words to finish this book. During the writing, I endured what seems to be the beginning stages of carpal tunnel. Nevertheless, the good Lord kept me going and He did NOT allow my wrist pain to stop me from reaching the finish line. We all have a goal. We can continue when life gets tough, or we can choose to quit. I pray you will always continue.

I truly hope everything covered in this book will continue to assist you throughout the rest of your life and you are willing to tell your family and friends about it. Sharing what you have learned will not only benefit you by allowing you to continue implementing the tools, but it will also help others who may be struggling in certain areas. Be blessed and stay in touch! I am always here if you need anything or have any questions about any of the topics discussed in this book. Feel free to reach out anytime.

Now it's time to Reclaim Your LIFE!

Your friend and advisor,

Jodi Watkins
www.2bepicfn.com
jodiwatkins@2bepicfn.com

Photo By: Tori Watkins
©2019 All Rights Reserved
Okinawa, Japan

About the Author, Jodi Watkins

My name is Jodi Watkins. I grew up in a small town called Fernandina Beach, right north of Jacksonville, Florida. I began my health journey after my third knee surgery and a couple years after having my daughter. I decided I wanted to learn more about nutrition and how to maintain a healthy lifestyle. I spent a total of 15 years in the United States Air Force. It was during that time that I developed my passion for helping others.

Over the past few years, I accomplished many things. However, I kept thinking about what I had not accomplished and the failures. I did not allow myself to cherish the successes. This ended in a downward spiral and a ton of depression. I finally got to the point where enough was enough. I had to learn how to turn the mirror around. I had to become aware of why I was allowing things in my past to dictate my present outcome. I had to truly develop a mindset of self-love and self-worth. I also had to understand the failures were not negative aspects of my life. They all set me up for where I am now. Everything that happened to me happened for me. While it took me this long to truly figure that out, I am grateful to have allowed myself to understand that concept and use it as fuel to help other women who may be going through similar situations or allowing their past to limit their future.

Through my own life experiences and knowledge acquired along the way, came this book.

I am now sharing the tools that took me years to learn and endure so others can free from themselves from their own limitations. I am truly passionate about helping parents by giving them these tools to pass down to their children and generations to follow. I encourage women and men to become the person they were always meant to be. Let's create a new destiny for next generation while feeling encouraged and empowered to live a life of total health and fulfillment!

My vision is to build a community where men and women feel supported in their goals and where new relationships and friendships develop. None of us are meant to go at this life alone and the Lord our God says, *"where two or three gather in my name, there I am with them"* (Matthew 18:20). That is His promise to us! So, what is stopping you! Let's become limitless together! It begins here.